WHAT OTHERS ARE SAYING

This book is not just informative, provocative, delightful. It is life-saving for churches and pastors who must navigate a world where the demonic and the divine have both been democratized to the point where any one person has the power of royalty to release good or evil on the rest of us. #ChoiceAndConsequences

— *Leonard Sweet,* best-selling author, professor, founder of preaching website preachthestory.com

This book explores, richly, beautifully, compelling, an intriguing idea: that the explosive growth of social media has put into all of our hands, literally, the kind of power and knowledge that once only royalty had. We can destroy a life with one Facebook post. We can disrupt massive institutions with a single tweet. We can reach audiences around the world by just pressing send on Instagram. Bryce Ashlin-Mayo isn't denouncing any of this. But he is calling for wisdom. But even better – he's providing such wisdom. This book, urgently needed, is so clear and helpful that anyone who reads it will learn how to use their regal power to do good, and not to harm.

— *Mark Buchanan,* award-winning author, professor at Ambrose University

In Age of Kings, Bryce gives us a fresh take on the life of King David that meets the needs of today's social media culture. Sharing compelling stories and rich insights, Bryce reminds us that we can find answers to the questions of our present and future by diving deep into the biblical stories and metaphors of our past. A valuable read to navigate our current culture well!

— *Beth Stovell,* Old Testament professor at Ambrose University; National Catalyst for Vineyard Canada and author of Minor Prophets I and II

This book is nothing short of brilliant in its analysis of how the world of social media can, paradoxically, both control its users, and yet give them a sense of empowerment at the same time. Thankfully, it is equally brilliant in its use of the biblical narrative of King David to articulate how the user of social media may wisely, safely, and righteously live in that world. The author's heart and concern for his readers come through clearly. It is delightfully written, and I have learned a great deal from it. I recommend this book highly.

— *Jerry Shepherd, Associate Professor of Old Testament at Taylor Seminary*

For those wise enough to engage it, Age of Kings provides a rare, skillful, and fruitful blend of cultural and biblical analysis. In the face of the seeming tangle of opportunities and challenges provided by the emerging social media culture, Ashlin-Mayo draws on the stories of Israel's King David to deliver to contemporary readers both biblical perspective and godly direction in their attempt to navigate well the tricky terrain of this brave new world. This well-written and approachable volume will serve as an invaluable resource for everyone who desires to live faithfully in the emerging and ever-shifting digital world.

— *Bernie A. Van De Walle, Professor of Historical and Systematic Theology at Ambrose University*

What does it mean to follow Christ in our social media age of Facebook and Twitter? In Age of Kings, Bryce Ashlin-Mayo offers us a wonderful answer with biblically grounded reflections on the life of David enriched by the wisdom of Solomon. An indispensable resource!

— *Randal Rauser, Professor of Historical Theology at Taylor Seminary and author of The Swedish Atheist, the Scuba Diver and Other Apologetic Rabbit Trails*

Bryce clearly engages the intersection of scripture and culture with winsome skill. This timely, excellent release is full of rich insights, cleverly explored. I'll buy copies for my youth leaders, as well as my own teenagers, since I'll be greedily clinging to my own. I recommend it 10/10!

— **David McDonald,** *Westwinds Church. Founder, The Fossores Chapter House: A Headquarters for Christian Ministerial Innovation www.doctordavidmcdonald.com, www.fossoreschapterhouse.com*

Age of Kings: Pursuing God's Heart in a Social Media World will guide you in the always-changing terrain of social media. This is a practical, helpful, and engaging guide for any age and I found myself highlighting early and often. Dr. Ashlin-Mayo sums up his work with this quote, "As followers of Jesus, may we stand tall and reach further, running on mission together, empowered by the opportunities and abilities that social media provides." A solid read!

— **Shane Sebastian,** *Executive Director, Cru*

In Age of Kings, Bryce Ashlin-Mayo weaves stories of kings and queens, giants and warriors, and even trolls, into a vivid tapestry picture of all our journeying through an increasingly complex and treacherous digital world. The book is elegantly written while paradoxically packing a visceral punch. Best of all though, Age of Kings calls every Jesus-formed man and woman to live out their divine calling faithfully, and with pastoral care Bryce provides wise and biblical counsel in how to do so.

— **Phillip G. Carnes,** *Executive Leadership Coach*

In Age of Kings, Dr. Ashlin-Mayo invites us to re-imagine the way we (as Christians) engage social media. Through rich metaphors and unique insights we are reminded of the fictions we tell about ourselves that are enacted and promoted through the selective editing of our lives on social media. The solution may be challenging, but his antidote better enables us to use the tools God has given us for good.

— *Thomas Ingram,* author of The New Normal

When it comes to social media, many use it, but few have thought through it. Bryce writes on a subject with theological depth, sociological astuteness, and insight into the Bible, culture, and the human heart that is so timely and needed.

— *Doug Witherup,* Lead Pastor of Concord First Assembly, Author of Interrobang Preaching

AGE OF KINGS

Pursuing God's Heart in a Social Media World

King Leon & Queen Rhonda

God Bless,

Bryce Ashlin-Mayo

incipiosermo
beginningconversation

Incipiosermo Press   incipiosermo.com

Age of Kings: Pursuing God's Heart in a Social Media World

Scriptures taken from the Holy Bible,
New International Version ®, NIV ®. Copyright © 1973, 1978,
1984, 2011 by Biblica, Inc.™ Used by permission of Zondervan.
All rights reserved worldwide. www.zondervan.com The "NIV"
and "New International Version" are trademarks registered in
the United States Patent and Trademark Office by Biblica, Inc.™

ISBN: 978-1-9994741-0-2 (softcover)
ISBN: 978-1-9994741-1-9 (electronic version)

Bryce Ashlin-Mayo
bryceashlinmayo.com
bryce@bryceashlinmayo.com
bryceashlinmayo@gmail.com

Incipiosermo Press
incipiosermo.com

DEDICATION

To my children (Nathanial, Sydney, and Lucas), may you
follow Jesus and pursue His heart in our social media world.
To Rob Parker, a hesed-friend through thick and thin.

ACKNOWLEDGEMENTS

Thank you to everyone who helped make this book possible.

Thank you to my wife, who encouraged me along the way. You are a true gift, my best friend, and my life-long partner. Thank you for saying yes on our wedding day and for supporting me every day since.

Thank you to my friends, colleagues, and various professionals who helped me in my craft and encouraged me to keep writing (Laurie Ashlin-Mayo, Hannah Ayer, Ken Badley, Ken Born, Mark Buchanan, Gregory Kline, Rob Parker, Colin Toffelmire, Ryan Tuck, and Doug Witherup).

Thank you to those who read advance copies of this book and offered helpful encouragement and thoughtful critique. It is much better as a result.

CONTENTS

PREFACE

This book is built upon years of reflection and study about technology and faith.[1] But this isn't just an exercise in intellectual curiosity; this book also represents my pastoral heart and my desire to see people follow Jesus faithfully and pursue His mission in the world.

Because of information technology and social media, we live in a time in which the power, knowledge, and platforms that were once available only to kings and queens can now be available to everyone. Power has been decentralized — so that it's no longer top-down — and democratized — so that it's no longer in the hands of only a few. This means that we all have been entrusted with power, and yet few of us are equipped to wield it successfully or ethically.

Much like a young crown prince or princess whose royal parent passes away unexpectedly, we've been thrust into power without adequate preparation. We have inherited a throne given to us by technology, and it has a world-wide platform and a reservoir of knowledge that we are unprepared to steward. The crown of our social media age has been given to us, and we have yet to grow into it. It's slipped over our eyes and blinded us — we are ignorant to what social media is doing to society and how it is affecting us.

As relatively new social media and information-technology users, we are still in our infancy; for all infants, learning to walk and run takes time, and it leaves bumps and scars along the way. As a father of three great kids, I remember when each of them learned to walk. At some point they understood

1

that walking was a more efficient way of getting around than crawling. With their mom and dad's help, they each took their first steps. They would first learn to stabilize on their feet, building their core and leg muscles. Once their muscles had strengthened, we would hold their hands as they stumbled along. And then, as they grew more confident, they would begin to walk independently, with one hand on the furniture, until they took their first independent steps and found freedom. Like all children, they wobbled, stumbled, and fell as they learned to walk. Wobbling, stumbling, and falling are all part of the process of learning and adjusting.

Today, each of us is learning to walk in a new technological landscape. We have been thrust into this new world and we are learning how to navigate it effectively. It isn't surprising that we would stumble at first as we build the muscles needed to stand, walk, and — eventually — run in our new world. As we do, we will find a new equilibrium, and we will adjust to the new power that we hold in the age of social media.

I have a few pre-emptive cautions for you as you read this book.

First, I want to be clear from the outset that I am not against social media. Although I would caution my kids and protect them from hitting their heads or falling on concrete as they learned to walk, I'm certainly not against walking! In the same way, I want to address the ways in which I think we are stumbling under the weight of our new-found power, but I believe that social media holds great promise and great possibilities. My hope is that this book would help raise awareness of some of the potential hazards of social media, while also giving a hopeful vision of its promise for God's mission in our world.

Second, in naming this book *Age of Kings*, I run the risk of seeming patriarchal. The language in the book is intentionally gender-inclusive (kings and queens) but the title reflects the reality of the Old Testament texts we will explore. We are living with challenges similar to what King David faced in the biblical age of kings.

Third, this book is not an in-depth study of the life of David. Rather, it uses short vignettes from the life and reign of David as descriptive examples of someone who, through his virtue and vices, lived with royal power and was still known as a man after God's heart.

I trust that you will learn some new things about our social media world as you read this book, but most of all I hope that you will gain insight and develop new ideas from the way that I apply the example of King David to our age. I might look at social media through a critical lens, but because I always have Jesus in view, my vision, at its heart, is hopeful.

I pray that this book will serve as a means to hold your hands as you learn to stand, walk, and run in our social media world, so that you can stay on mission with Jesus. I trust that it will help to equip and empower you to grow into the crown of power that social media has imparted upon each of us. It is my prayerful desire that we might leverage our royal power for the King of Kings, Jesus Christ.

INTRODUCTION
The Age of Kings

As someone born in the mid-seventies, I have lived through the digital revolution, including the invention of the cell phone, the personal computer, the internet, and social media. In my relatively short lifetime, I have seen the telephone evolve from a large, bulky device permanently mounted on a wall to a hand-held device that can be stowed securely in my pocket, while at the same time it serves as a computer, a word processor, an encyclopedia, a shopping mall, a camera, and a stereo.

This digital revolution has implications for real life. It affects all aspects of life and culture — from national security down to awkward adolescent romances. When I was in high school, "texting" a girl meant passing a note in class through the hands of nosey classmates in a desperate effort to find out if she "liked you" or "*liked* liked you." It wasn't that long ago that friends had to come over to your house to look at photobooks full of overexposed

Our world is vibrating with the frequency of change.

pictures (probably taken on a disposable camera) to find out how your vacation was. Only close friends would care enough to go to the trouble. In the days before IMDb, a disagreement with your friends over which actor was in a particular movie could turn into a lengthy argument with no obvious winner. In the last forty years, technology has radically evolved, and as a result it has changed the way we interact with each other and the way our society functions.

Our world is vibrating with the frequency of change. Social media and information technology have disrupted the way we understand and interpret our world, and that has fundamentally changed our understandings of reality, authority, community, relationships, and power structures. This disruption and reordering are echoed subversively in the nursery rhyme Humpty Dumpty:

> *Humpty Dumpty sat on a wall,*
> *Humpty Dumpty had a great fall.*
> *All the king's horses and all the king's men*
> *Couldn't put Humpty together again.*
>
> *–Mother Goose*

The rhyme doesn't tell us who or what Humpty Dumpty is. For some unknown reason, this unknown person or object falls to its demise and breaks apart and is unable to be put back together again, even with the help of an army.

But what if Humpty Dumpty is the king himself? That would, at the very least, explain why *all* the king's horses and *all* the king's men were sent out to put Humpty back together again.

I'd like to consider how, in our time, the introduction of

5

so much new technology has shaken the foundations of our culture — our kingdom. To use the imagery of the nursery rhyme, this means that our king who was once secure is now shattered on the ground. But what if the introduction of a new technology not only shifted the once-secure wall and the once-secure king, but also fragmented the king's power into many pieces, and every person in the kingdom now holds a piece? Democratization like this would surely alter the power structure and culture of the entire kingdom forever.

As social media and information technology play an increasingly large role in our culture and our consciousness, they dismantle our walls — our understanding of the world, our categories, our hierarchies, our relational norms, our power structures — and rebuild them according to a new blueprint. Like the broken king, the old walls can't be put back together again.

This means that we won't find a new normal by returning our culture to the way it was. Instead, we must reform and adjust to the new way of things and the new, more democratic distribution of power. But in order to follow through with this reformation and adjustment, the citizens of our kingdom need new skills and different abilities.

We're sitting on a new wall, and we're being drawn onward into a new age: The age of kings and queens.

Drawn Onward

"Are we not drawn onward, we few, drawn onward to new era?"[2] This famous palindrome (a word or phrase that can be read backwards the same as it can forwards) also carries a hidden

message that's particularly prophetic for our age. Whether we like it or not, we are drawn onward into this new social media era, but this new era carries with it echoes of the past. We will find meaning for our era by looking ahead, but we will also find meaning for it by looking backward.

It is often assumed that the world we are entering is a new frontier, and that we're untethered from the past. As a result, history, literature, and biblical insights can end up being dismissed as obsolete. However, what if our hubris has blinded us to the lessons of the past?

A number of years ago NASA faced the problem of efficiently and effectively transporting and deploying solar arrays on their satellites. They tried countless new techniques and explored many new and emerging technologies, but still they were unable to find an efficient way to pack the solar arrays for launch and release them effectively in orbit. The engineers were stumped.

Learning from King David's successes and failures, we can glean hope for living life with the power of kings and queens.

Finally, in desperation, a NASA scientist relied on some old wisdom, or, as he put it, "letting dead people do your work for you;" he took his problem and turned it "into a problem that someone else has solved." [3] Taking a lesson from ancient Japanese culture and the art-form of origami, NASA found a way to fold their solar arrays efficiently and deploy them effectively in orbit.

The future of satellite solar arrays was made possible not by a new discovery but because of an ancient art form. The way forward was found through a rediscovery of the past. Sometimes the lessons we need to learn are not found in the new but in the old, if we can repurpose them for a new era.

Therefore, when it comes to learning to follow Jesus faithfully in our digital, high-tech, and social media world, the
Bible is not an obsolete source. The biblical authors might
have been ignorant on the subject of the internet, but that
doesn't mean that their insights are irrelevant for us. Rather,
the Bible contains timeless lessons that are truly relevant for
a world in which we all have the power, temptations, and
opportunities that once belonged only to kings and queens.

This is why the person and kingship of David are excep-
tionally relevant. Characterized as a person after God's heart
(1 Samuel 13:14), David, through his virtues and vices, is our
best example of a powerful person learning to follow God.
Learning from King David's successes and failures, we can
glean hope for living life with the power of kings and queens.

To be clear, the life and reign of King David is not an
example of perfection or excellence; rather, it is a narrative
of God's faithfulness and one person's journey to try and
follow God faithfully with the new power entrusted to them.
David's life and challenges bear a surprising resemblance to
the reality we face today. The king after God's own heart has
timeless truth to impart to a people — you and me — who
desire to follow Jesus in our new world, filled with the power
of royalty and yet labouring under the weight of it.

The Map of the Kingdom

This book is filled with hope and practical biblical teaching
for followers of Jesus in our social media world. Journeying
chronologically through the life of David, this book unfolds
eight lessons that can be applied to our emerging age of

kings and queens.

Chapter 1 presents the anointing of David as the future king and explores the notion that the Age of Kings is an age of personal propaganda. Social media has empowered everyone with the ability to edit, shape, and broadcast their personal narrative to the world, which has provided the average person with a temptation once experienced only by royalty: the temptation to personal propaganda.

Chapter 2 looks at the story of David and Goliath to illuminate how the Age of Kings is an age of #hashtivism. Utilizing the metaphor of compassion fatigue, this chapter tackles the unique dynamic of #hashtivism and suggests practical steps to combat the apathy that can be a side-effect of hearing social media's endless calls for intervention against the backdrop of our limited resources.

Chapter 3 explores the relationship of David and Jonathan as a means to understand the Age of Kings as an age of acquaintances. Paradoxically, in an age in which people are more connected than ever before, people are feeling more alone. This paradox might seem unique to our time, but it is something often felt by people with great power. With practical application, this chapter will examine the Hebrew word *hesed* to discover the lessons it holds for our relationships in our hyper-connected and acquaintance-filled world.

Chapter 4 uses the story of David sparing Saul's life as an instructive tale to help us navigate the Age of Kings as an age of trolls. Social media gives everyone a megaphone. This vignette from David's life highlights practical ways to reject vitriol and revenge, and instead to use our newfound power to build up and foster life rather than to destroy it.

Chapter 5 unpacks the narrative of David bringing the ark

back to Jerusalem in order to explain the Age of Kings as an age of selfies. On social media, anyone can promote themselves in unprecedented fashion, and in the age of the selfie we have traded our pursuit of God's glory for the elevation and glory of ourselves. This chapter shares a subversive alternative possibility for a culture that's obsessed with relentless self-promotion and the exhausting pursuit of fame.

Chapter 6 looks at the story of David and Bathsheba in order to examine the implications of the Age of Kings being an age of desire. Information technology and social media grant us access to any image or video at any time. Although technology didn't create the temptation to lust, it did give us the unique power to fulfill our sexual desires instantly, and this power was once available only to kings and queens. This reality is radically altering our relationships and our views of sex, as well as our sexual ethics, behaviours, and expectations. With practical application, this chapter shows how we can resist this temptation by being faithful to our calling.

Chapter 7 explores the narrative of David being confronted by the prophet Nathan and the reality that the Age of Kings is an age of cognification. Social media and information technology leverage algorithms and machine-learning to help us wade through the sea of information and find what we need, but they also anticipate and gratify our desires. This chapter explores this implication of power and presents a way to counteract its potential negative impact.

Chapter 8 examines the narrative of David hearing news of victory in battle alongside news of his son's death in order to unpack the reality that our Age of Kings is an age of fake news. Social media has given everyone a voice and it has amplified all those voices without discernment or judgement.

Thanks to this, the internet is awash with false claims, and we're now facing an era of fake news and the confirmation bias that feeds it. This chapter unravels the challenge of sifting through unfiltered information in order to discern fact from fiction.

The book closes with the last words of David. The conclusion summarizes the themes of the book and presents a vision for faithfully pursing God's heart in the Age of Kings, a vision filled with hope and life.

The Journey Ahead

A couple years ago, when our children were in elementary school, our family went on one of our long hikes on a mountain trail. What began as a simple trek through gentle terrain soon became difficult. I still remember trying to guide my young children along the path. I held their hands as they awkwardly stumbled along the rocks and slippery mud, keeping them safe while we made slow and methodical progress along the trail.

This is how I view my role as author. I hope to guide you on a journey through the life of David in an effort to guide you in our ever-changing digital terrain. My goal is not to avoid the difficult path ahead but rather to use the Bible as our compass and to grab Jesus' hands so that together we can navigate the terrain in a way that honours Him. The path into our social media world might pretty quickly go from easy to difficult, but we can navigate it, and, like the view that greeted my family at the end of our arduous hike, the destination of our social media journey is beautiful. When we've learned how to use social media to honour Jesus and engage in His mission in the world, we'll feel that it was worth the journey!

To aid the journey ahead, each chapter begins by making observations and surveying the terrain of our social media age. The chapter then looks at the life and reign of David as told in 1 and 2 Samuel to illuminate truths about living faithfully as kings and queens. Each chapter then concludes with practical help and a hopeful vision for following Jesus faithfully in this new social media world. Further to that, at the end of each chapter you will find the Royal Reflec-

If there is hope for King David, there is hope for kings and queens like you and me.

tion. This section is filled with reflection questions and response suggestions that invite you to understand more deeply and apply your understanding to your life. Each Royal Reflection recommends a psalm that's connected to the David story used in the chapter.

Although life in the Age of Kings is filled with both promise and peril, the life of David echoes with hope. His story shows us that it is possible for kings and queens to pursue God's heart.

If there is hope for King David, there is hope for kings and queens like you and me.

PERSONAL PROPAGANDA

My family and I are fortunate enough to live just a short drive from the Canadian Rocky Mountains. These majestic mountain ranges are a hiking destination for visitors from all over the world. To take full advantage of our locale, from time to time — and with varying degrees of protest from our children — my wife and I organize a family hike in the Rockies.

All these excursions begin the same way: after an intense and debatably-successful reverse hostage-negotiation to get our teenagers *out* of the house and *into* our van on a Saturday morning, we hit the road later than planned. The hour-long drive is filled with family angst, annoying dad jokes, disagreements, laughs, and healthy doses of Ashlin-Mayo-branded sarcasm.

Once we arrive at our destination and begin our trek, I take out my phone to capture the gorgeous views, unintentional and blurry photos of feet, pictures of my kids walking together joyously, and snapshots of our family in various expressions of disgust and discontentment.

After the hike, as my wife drives us back, I sit in the passenger seat and reflect on the day with the help of my phone. I sort through the photos I captured, beginning the process of creating a social media post to share our experience with the world.

Guess which pictures I deem worthy of posting?

I inevitably pick the best shots of the day, both in terms of relative photographic quality and in terms of the expressions of enjoyment the shots capture. I either delete the remaining pictures or leave them to lie dormant on my phone. Then, once I've touched up the best photos — cropped them, adjusted the brightness and colours, added filters, etc. — I post them to my social media channels and anxiously anticipate the reactions and responses from my followers.

Now, it isn't that the photos I shared were inaccurate; however, they definitely showed the world a carefully edited view of the day. Anyone who glanced at them would be led to assume — falsely — that our day was spectacular in every way, devoid of strife, frustration, and disappointment.

This ubiquitous contemporary practice of sharing our self-edited narratives with the world might seem like a new, unique feature of our lives today, but in fact it is merely a version of a practice employed by kings and queens of old: propaganda.

Propaganda

People of power, like kings and queens, are often guilty of spreading propaganda. Propaganda, according to the Merriam-Webster definition, is the intentional offering of information that has been edited or even skewed to offer a particular (and possibly false) view of the world.

In some cases — like with the photos of happy family poses and walks in the park propagated by Prince William and Catherine, Duchess of Cambridge — propaganda can seem essentially innocuous. But in nefarious hands — Hitler and the Nazi regime are the classic example — it can be truly insidious. This ability of the wealthy and powerful to propagate a carefully edited narrative in order to influence public opinion in their favour has been democratized by social media. The power once held by a select few is now held by the masses, as are the temptations that power brings. As a result, we are now all potential propagandists, selectively editing our stories and sharing them through our social media platforms.

We are now all potential propagandists, selectively editing our stories.

Image Management

Whether it is through the image and persona one conveys on Facebook or the skills, experience, connections, and endorsements one accumulates on LinkedIn, image matters in our culture. The rapid growth of personal propaganda on social media has made way for new fields of employment designed to help the average person propagate their preferred image to the world. One of these is the image consultant. Today, people willingly pay professionals to help them manicure and curate their social media lives to portray success and power, with the hope and promise of greater opportunities and even greater success.

One of the challenges of image management is that image

moves in two directions simultaneously. First, our self-edited image reflects what we want others to see in us, portraying our lives through the flattering lens of success and achievement, often void of the failures, mistakes, pain, and sorrow that occur in every life. Second, other people's images are directed at us: we view the edited projected lives of others as real and authentic; even though we thoroughly edit our own

When we take the personal propaganda that others share as true and accurate and we compare it to the reality we live, we are almost guaranteed to feel inadequate and dissatisfied.

stories before we post them, we somehow don't assume that others have done the same. This means that we unfairly compare our known realities — the flawed, unfiltered ones — to the carefully touched-up versions of life that other people project. When we take the personal propaganda that others share as true and accurate and we compare it to the reality we live, we are almost guaranteed to feel inadequate and dissatisfied. And that can be destructive.

Narcissus

This reality is illustrated in the Greek myth of Narcissus. To state the myth simply, Narcissus abruptly leaves the infatuated Echo, which breaks her heart. Nemesis, the goddess of revenge, decides to punish Narcissus for his cruelty to Echo, so she lures him to a brook and shows him his reflection in the water. He falls in love with his own image, and eventually his self-obsession leads him to drown.

In our language today, *nemesis* refers to our arch-enemy

and *narcissism* is the obsession with the self. These two words that originate in this story pair well in the appetite of our culture.

Social media makes us increasingly susceptible to the temptation of our cultural nemesis: narcissism. Like Narcissus, we've been lured to the water's edge and sit transfixed by our own reflections.

Inspired by the work of the late Canadian media theorist Marshall McLuhan, I suggest that Narcissus didn't fall in love with himself but rather with a distorted reflection of himself. As we know, water reflects an image not exactly as it is, but slightly distorted from the real thing.[4] Through social media, we have fallen in love with ourselves and the lives of others; but the image we've fallen in love with is a distorted and altered version that reflects our self-editing and our filtered desires. This is so much the case that we are in danger of losing ourselves and drowning in our own distorted reflections.

As social media tempts us to personal propaganda, one of the chief targets of this propaganda is ourselves.

Consider the memories feature on social media platforms: the platform shows you a post from your own digital past to remind you of a moment in your history and prompt you to share that memory with your friends. As social media tempts us to personal propaganda, one of the chief targets of this propaganda is ourselves. If our memories are triggered only by positive and self-edited social media posts from our pasts, we can be tempted to compare our present selves with these self-edited and constructed versions from the past, and to idealize and even fall in love with these versions of ourselves. In essence, we are tempted not only to perpetrate propaganda but also to be its victim.

Recently, I had a memory pop up on my newsfeed. It was a photo that made it seem like all was right with the world. At first glance, the photo brought back to me the moment it had captured: the perfect sky, the smiling faces, and the warm feelings. But as I considered the memory more carefully, I remember that the day was also full of disappointment and anxiety over a situation I was in. Although the beauty that the picture captured was true, it was only one aspect of the day; the day only seemed perfect and sublime when I considered that one aspect outside of its context. If I had only paid attention to the positive aspects of that memory, like my social media was nudging me to, I would have neglected to remember the angst and disappointment of the day and the hope I experienced in the midst of it. The angst of the day is a fundamental part of the story that is shaping me, and I would have forgotten all about it if I had recalled only the positive memory that I had shared as part of my own personal propaganda. When we gaze at our distorted reflections — our edited memories and false comparisons — we might conclude that our present can't compare to our past. We can drown in our own reflections.

> **When we gaze at our distorted reflections — our edited memories and false comparisons — we might conclude that our present can't compare to our past. We can drown in our own reflections.**

David's Story Is Our Story

If this is our reality, how can we follow God faithfully? How can we overcome the temptation to propagandize and stop comparing our realities to the idealized projections of others? We can find an answer in the story of King David, specifically in how and why he was chosen by God to be king. As we will discover, God's selection criteria are not met by outward appearances but by what matters to God: the heart.

Learning from the Life of King David
1 Samuel 16:1–13

David's story begins as King Saul's story takes a turn toward its inevitable and ignoble end. As Saul's kingship unravels, Samuel is secretly sent by God to anoint the next king of Israel.

When the Israelites ask God for a king, they're looking for the classic image of a strong and dominant leader. They see physical appearance and strength as the standard for royal success. Saul has all the outward characteristics that the people covet, and as such they accept and celebrate him as their leader.

However, as time progresses, Saul's veneer of success and strength fractures and eventually is stripped from him. He caves to temptation and can't overcome difficulties; he continually fails the leadership and character challenges that come his way. However, Saul reaches his demise not only because of his personal character flaws, many of which David shares, but because he is selfishly disinterested in following God's leading for Israel. Saul's crisis of character and his wilful ignorance of God's leading for the nation move God to call upon the prophet Samuel to anoint a new King of Israel. God leads Samuel to the farm of a man named Jesse to find a successor among Jesse's sons.

The sons are presented to Samuel, and there are a few who seem to have the royal look, but God doesn't indicate a royal successor among them. Finally, Jesse calls for his youngest son to come from the field.

When David appears, fresh from the field and probably a bit worse for wear, God says to Samuel, "Rise and anoint him; this is the one" (1 Samuel 16:12). Samuel then anoints David with oil as the future king and the Holy Spirit falls on him. David is chosen not because of his image and exterior appearance — although he does possess health and good looks — but because of the state of his heart.

If, however, we place our identity and worth in the hands of Jesus, we receive our value from His eternal, perfect, and sustaining love.

There is a vital lesson for all of us in this story. To follow God faithfully in an age of kings and queens, we must allow the Holy Spirit to transform our obsession with external image into a concern for our inner lives, values, and character. God is not looking for people with perfectly manicured lives on the exterior; rather, He is looking for people whose inner lives are focused on Him, and who display integrity between their interior and exterior lives as a result. These are the core qualities that will help us to perceive that our reflections in the water are not clear but distorted, and to stand up from the water's edge and faithfully follow Jesus on the path He has for us.

As followers of Jesus in a social media world, may we

re-centre our lives on Jesus and may we pursue His path with a renewed sense of identity, authenticity, and integrity, pointing towards God in humility. These are key values that are often ignored in a social media world that elevates opinions devoid of fact, images devoid of substance, and success devoid of love.

Pursuing God's Heart in a Social Media World

It is far from easy to pursue God's heart in the new Age of Kings. It demands that we intentionally realign our hearts, pull our eyes up from our intoxicating but distorted reflections, and fix our gaze firmly on Jesus, the author and perfecter of our faith (Hebrews 12:2). By adding simple disciplines into our routines, we can constantly remind ourselves of our propensity to propagandize and our need to embrace truth and grace in our lives and in the lives of others. To that end, we are invited to find our identity and worth in Jesus intentionally and to share our lives with others with authenticity and integrity.

Affirm Your Worth and Identity

The age of kings and queens can create an obsession with following others and having others follow us. This obsession places value on what others think of us and how we think of ourselves based on comparing our real lives with the self-edited lives of others. These values tempt us to base our identity on others' perceptions of us.

When we place our identity and worth in the hands of others, we submit our value to their fragile and fickle embrace. This can leave us feeling insecure, which makes us vulnerable to manipulation and control. People who have a selfish agenda tend to play on other people's insecurity; in fact, advertisers and politicians intentionally leverage this tendency in an attempt to influence our decisions and actions.

According to one study, forty-six percent of all women feel less attractive on Mondays. [5] This study wasn't commissioned to help women reverse this insecurity but rather to help marketers and advertisers to prey more effectively upon it. Marketers and advertisers of cosmetics products solicited this data and used it to target their ads to women when they would be most susceptible to the product pitch. This is just one example of those who would leverage our fears and insecurities for their own selfish ends. When we place our identity and worth in the hands of others, we are at our most vulnerable.

If, however, we place our identity and worth in the hands of Jesus, we receive our value from His eternal, perfect, and sustaining love. Jesus' perfect love, and the secure identity that we find in Him, sets us free from the temptation to compare ourselves to others and instead empowers us to love Jesus fully in return. It also gives us the strength to love others.

Where is your identity and worth formed? Is it formed by fickle social media fame or is it found in the deep, trustworthy, and abundant love of Jesus? Ephesians 3:14–19 reminds us of our identity and worth in Christ, where we are loved with a love that is deeper, wider, longer, and higher than anything we can imagine. In Jesus, we no longer need to be loved by others to find our identity and worth; rather, the power of the Holy Spirit strengthens us deep within our inner being. Our inner being is where our identity is formed, rooted, and established in God's unfailing love.

As a pastor, when I have people in my office seeking direction over an issue or struggling with guilt and shame about something, I often guide the conversation along these lines. I ask them, "What do you think Jesus would say to you right now?" As they answer, they often tell me about Jesus confronting them on their sin or about Jesus telling them not to be worried about their decision. Not to dispute the content of their response, but I usually challenge their initial assertions by offering an alternative. I remind them, regardless of their circumstances, that I believe that the first thing Jesus would say to them is that they are loved, that He profoundly and lavishly loves them. Often, upon hearing this truth, the person breaks down in tears or smiles in reception of the reminder.

In our world of wavering and conditional 'love,' we need regular reminders of the truth: that God's love is unwavering and unconditional.

In our world of wavering and conditional 'love,' we need regular reminders of the truth: that God's love is unwavering and unconditional. It needs nothing from us to secure it; it is outside our control. For propagandists, this is often overwhelming but extremely good news. God does want to free us from our sin and guide us in our decisions, but He always does so in the context of His extravagant love.

In this age of kings and queens, an identity is offered to you by social media, but this identity cannot deliver the things it promises. Instead, embrace the identity you have as a follower of Jesus. This identity is not based on how many followers you have on Twitter, how many "likes" your post or profile picture has on Facebook, how many contacts you have on LinkedIn, or even what others think about you and your life. Rather, it's found in God's unfailing love.

Post Authentically

In this age of propaganda, we're constantly tempted to share our self-edited stories with the world in hopes of gaining approval and acclaim. Faced with that temptation, one of the most counter-cultural, subversive, and beautiful things we can do is to intentionally practice authenticity. We can do this by rejecting the temptation to propagandize and choosing instead to post and share with radical honestly about the realness of life (in appropriately transparent detail).

One of the most prophetically radical things we can do in our social media world is to find authentic beauty in the seemingly ordinary and share it with the world.

There is a trend in our culture, sparked by personal propaganda, that celebrates the "extraordinary" with a corresponding disdain for the "ordinary." This way of thinking encourages us to discard and devalue the so-called ordinary things of life, as if ordinariness were a defect. Ordinary is underrated. One of the most prophetically radical things we can do in our social media world is to find authentic beauty in the seemingly ordinary and share it with the world.

What if we intentionally pulled back the curtains of our lives to reveal the truth of our ordinariness? That would be an extraordinary display of authenticity.

It is a beautifully subversive thing to live authentically in an age of propaganda. Our world is in desperate need of the real and the ordinary; it needs a prophetic display of authenticity. Make it a regular practice to post the real, ordinary things of your life and to recognize and celebrate the ordinary in the lives of the people in your social media networks.

Practice Integrity

Integrity is the practice of living the same way in public as you live in private. Living in the social-media age of kings and queens, with the temptation to propagandize your story, your public, social-media life might look distinctly different from your private life. In fact, the medium of social media allows us all to abuse this power in unprecedented ways.

Consider the phenomenon of *catfishing*. Catfishing is the nefarious social media tactic of taking on a different identity on social media in order to attract a particular individual or kind of person. Many of the stories I hear of catfishing are born out of insecurity and romantic hopes: for instance, people who catfish on dating apps portray themselves falsely in a desperate attempt to find love, hoping that their false identity will get them a date, and that, eventually, their real personality will secure a relationship. Catfishing is, essentially, an extreme version of the subtle deceptions we all practice in one way or another.

It is so easy for us to deceive the outside world. The temptation is great for us as kings and queens in the age of propaganda to portray our lives in ways that deceive, either by addition or by omission. Although it is appropriate to hide certain parts of our lives because of the need for personal privacy, it is dishonest and deceptive to build a falsified version of our lives that is untethered from reality.

As you post and share, always seek to be faithful and true in the words you share and the stories you tell.

What if the story I told at the beginning of this chapter had a slightly different ending? What if in my carefully filtered post-hiking social media post I included an intentionally raw and authentic family photo as an act of subversive honesty? Or, what if I decided not to post any photo that makes my family look different than it really is? This might not change the world in and of itself, but it might help take a small step towards reclaiming my authentic identity.

Therefore, as you post, make it a discipline to intentionally ask yourself if what you are posting is true and free from both the dishonesty of addition and the dishonesty of omission. As Proverbs 11:3 says, "The integrity of the upright guides them, but the unfaithful are destroyed by their duplicity." If your post lacks integrity and honesty, ask yourself why you feel the temptation to post something that isn't true. Explore what that temptation might say about where you are finding your value, worth, and identity. As you post and share, always seek to be faithful and true in the words you share and the stories you tell.

A Hope-Filled Vision of Identity, Authenticity, and Integrity in the Age of Kings

Following Jesus faithfully in the Age of Kings means recognizing the truth that God looks at our hearts and inner lives rather than at our outward appearances. Consequently, it is imperative that we find and affirm our identity in Jesus, post authentically, and practice integrity. This is the remarkable potential of the digital age, the ability to highlight and share the transparent beauty of the ordinary in each of us. Imagine followers of Jesus telling the story of their real lives, with all its real doubts amidst real faith, in front of our world that is searching desperately — in all the wrong places — for a real, authentic story. This story is the story of Jesus, who transforms by His mercy and grace. May we use social media to tell this real, grace-filled, and Jesus-centred story.

Held captive by the delusions of our propaganda, we can begin to believe our own mythology. Instead, may we find our identity in Jesus and celebrate the freedom that true authenticity and integrity can bring and share it with the world.

A Royal Reflection

Read

- Psalm 89
- This psalm is written long after David's death and recounts David's anointing as king. Written during a bleak time in Israel's history by Ethan the Ezrahite, the psalm proclaims David's identity as the Lord's anointed, God's promise to him, and God's promises to his future generations.

Reflect

- As you post on social media, how do you find yourself participating in personal propaganda? How authentic are you online?

- Why do you struggle with authenticity and integrity online? Could part of your struggle be connected to where your identity is formed?
- What is your identity as a follower of Jesus, child of God, and son or daughter of the King Jesus? Make a list of who you are in Jesus (Examples: I am loved, I am forgiven, I am free, etc.). Place that list in your Bible so that you can regularly be reminded of this truth.

Respond

- This week, commit to doing a double-take on your social media posts. Ask yourself if they are authentic and true. If not, ask yourself why. What might that say about where you are getting your identity?
- This week, commit to posting a picture or statement that expresses a real and transparent part of your life.
- This week, commit to posting something that identifies the beauty in the authentic ordinary.

#HASHTIVISM

About ten years ago, traditional media *jumped the shark*[6] with advertisements aimed at engaging the public to help solve global problems such as disease, famine, and disaster. In the early days of television and radio ads, simple information-based television and radio appeals were used effectively by compassion and relief organizations to fundraise for their respective causes. However, as time went on and an increasing number of organizations leveraged this tool, it saturated the public consciousness and reduced the effectiveness of these appeals. As a result, organizations began to use more direct, personal, and emotionally-driven appeals, like those that featured visceral images with the faces of suffering children and animals. But eventually even this intense style of advertising lost its effectiveness. People have become so exhausted

Any person's micro-needs can be micro-financed by micro-targeting everyone they're connected to in the social media landscape.

by the endless stream of problems paraded before them in the media that they have been lulled into collective complacency.

Our world faces giant problems, and social media has only increased our awareness of them. Terrorists perpetually wage a borderless war that seems impossible to fight, the enemy difficult to define and isolate. Our climate is in crisis with potentially irreversible consequences. The global economy is in dangerous tension between globalization and individual countries' national interests. Social media confronts us with these giant problems every day.

Our compassion has withered in the shadow of the world's great and small needs.

But social media doesn't just amplify these huge global problems; it also magnifies the small challenges within our own social circles. Every day, our social media feeds remind us of the personal challenges that face our social media friends and followers and implore us to help solve these problems. Appeals for crowd-funding would have us support friends' missions trips, pay portions of medical bills for friends' family members, help launch new products, and replace stolen phones for mere acquaintances. Any person's micro-needs can be micro-financed by micro-targeting everyone they're connected to in the social media landscape.

The constant onslaught of disasters, needs, requests, and challenges can paralyze us with fear, anxiety, apathy, and guilt. We fear what could happen and what impact it could have on our individual lives, our families, our community, our country, and our world, and so we stick our heads in the sand. In fact, many professionals believe that this fear is at the root of our cultural anxiety; as we are faced with the constant bombardment of bad news about problems in our world, it increases our culture's depression and exacerbates our anxiety epidemic. In fact, experts say that being confronted constantly with bad news conjures up worry about the bad news and also provides fertile ground for unrelated worries to grow in our lives.[7] This anxiety, fueled by our fears, leads not to action but instead to apathy and guilt.

Over time, if our compassion has become fatigued, we probably respond with apathy. Faced by the flood of stories that demand our compassion, our hearts can become hard and we can end up protecting ourselves by being calculatedly cold and by strategically rationing our compassion. Finally, when our compassion falters, we are often stuck with guilt. Although guilt can be a powerful motivator, that kind of motivation is always short-lived. The short-term responses we make out of guilt might just leave us feeling guiltier.

As I've learned from parenting teenagers, guilt can elicit short-term change but does little to alter long-term behaviour. Parents can be experts in guilt. Every parent seems to know intrinsically how to use guilt to manipulate behaviour, but good parents know that if you are trying to make your child into the best human you can, guilt won't help you reach that goal. For example, if I want my kids to bring their dirty dishes out of their rooms every day (a common struggle for parents of teenagers), guilt might motivate them in the short-term, but ultimately it won't help to form them into responsible young adults. The same is true of our motivation for helping others. If we are being motivated by the guilt we feel about not doing something rather than by the transformative motivation of being part of God's kingdom mission, then we will keep feeling guiltier no matter what we do.

Now that all the brokenness of our world is laid bare through social media, we can be very tempted to isolate ourselves and to lurch back into bubbles of ignorance and inactivity, lulled into a state of seeming comfort and security, unaware of the lonely prisons we have created. In our age of kings and queens, our compassion has withered in the shadow of the world's great and small needs.

#Hashtivism

This reality is evidenced in the social media phenomenon known as *#Hashtivism*. This refers to the way social media users can tag an event, challenge, or systemic issue with a hashtag that can then be traced and followed online. The hope is usually that it will lead to societal and cultural change. Although this tactic can be used effectively to organize people into action, people most often use it simply to express their verbal support for a given side of an issue. This can give them the feeling that they no longer need to respond with action, as if words typed on a post are enough (hence the phenomenon's other name, *slacktivism*). When a huge chorus of voices is calling for attention on social media, a hashtag is more likely to serve as a convenient, passive conduit of response than as a true rallying cry.

For centuries, only the politically powerful regularly faced the dilemma of what to do in the face of endless need while there were limited resources in the treasury.

For centuries, only the politically powerful regularly faced the dilemma of what to do in the face of endless need while there were limited resources in the treasury. Famously, when faced with this choice, many of the politically powerful have chosen to benefit only themselves. But this is not a response that befits followers of Jesus. As the Apostle John says in 1 John 3:17-18, "If anyone has material possessions and sees a brother or sister in need but has no pity on them, how can the love of God be in that person? Dear children, let us not love with words or speech but with actions and in truth."

As a result of the democratized power created by social media, it is now our turn to hear the endless problems of our world while we also consider the limited resources at our disposal. As we hear the constant call of the challenges in our world, how will we respond?

David's Story Is Our Story

The age of kings and queens has made us come face to face with challenges of all sizes, all of which can taunt us as if they were giants that cannot be defeated. If we don't know how to respond to the taunting, we can look to young David, who in the company of King Saul and the Israelite army faced Goliath the giant. As these challenges call out to us, what is our response?

Learning from the Life of King David
1 Samuel 17:1–58

After David is secretly anointed as the next king, he returns to shepherding in the field. Later, he plays his music for King Saul to soothe the soul of the troubled king. He continues to perform his duties and to serve the king, awaiting God's timing for him to live out his anointed destiny.

In the Age of Kings, we can wait impatiently for God to put us in the context of our calling. We want things to happen now. We want our destiny to align immediately with our destination, but that is not how God often works. In God's slow and inefficient Kingdom, calling and destiny are often separated by the wilderness between now and then — the desert between promise and fulfillment.

It is during this very season of liminality that we find David serving his family. As David arrives on the frontlines of a battle in order to bring food to his brothers and their commander, he is greeted by a verbose giant on the horizon. Goliath, a warrior of great strength and apparently insurmountable power, has arrived to taunt the Israelites yet again to find an opponent worthy of him within their ranks.

At this point in its history, the kingdom of Israel is facing a literal giant as well as a figurative, existential one. Goliath is a problem for sure, but their bigger problem is the current king. The failed King Saul, whom even God has rejected, is paralyzed by fear and ignorant of God's power and potential to empower His people to victory.

The Philistines designate Goliath — a man of great stature, strength and power — as their warrior representative. Who do the Israelites choose?

If anyone should have fought Goliath as a representative of Israel, it should have been King Saul. Every Israelite knew who their designate should be. Saul, the once-victorious warrior king, is now paralyzed by fear. As we learn from the narrative, not only does Saul not believe in his own ability to fight the giant but, more importantly, he does not believe in God's power to lead and empower him to victory.

This deficiency in belief and faith is confronted and contrasted by young David. Gazing at the giant before him, David responds with righteous defiance and holy indignation, rooted in his confidence in God. David's courageous response is to volunteer to fight the giant as Israel's representative. King Saul is so impressed with David that he agrees to his outrageous offer.

In God's slow and inefficient Kingdom, calling and destiny are often separated by the wilderness between now and then — the desert between promise and fulfillment.

David, who doesn't even fit into the great Saul's armour, reminds us that God is the one who will be the victor in the story, not David. David leaves behind the armour and weapons of the king and takes the weapons he knows, which are the weapons of a shepherd. The one who killed lions and bears while protecting his sheep will now fight the giant as the protective shepherd King of Israel.

Throughout the narrative, the contrast between David and Saul deepens. Saul, whom the Israelites celebrated for his strength and kingly appearance, is now found to lack character, in contrast to David, a young shepherd boy whose confidence is not in his own abilities but in God's. This contrast reminds us again that although we may look at and value the exterior, God looks at the heart.

Walking to a nearby stream and picking up five smooth stones, David goes into battle with who he is, with what he has, and with a God who is all powerful before Him. Five stones are selected but only one is needed, as David takes down the well-armed and seemingly invincible giant with the first stone he casts from his simple sling. The giant who taunts Israel is no match for the God who fights injustice.

David's faith and confidence in God allow him the ability to see, understand, and engage with the giant problem before him with courage and boldness. Using what David had (his sling and stone) and who he was (a shepherd), God worked through David to conquer both the literal giant that taunted his future kingdom and the giant problem of an unfit ruler.

As illustrated in Saul, we can grow so overwhelmed that we choose inactivity in the face of problems that seem insurmountable. As kings and queens with our new-found social media power, may we learn the lesson from David and find our confidence and hope in God. As we do, we can leverage God's power, resources, and influence for all God wants to do in our broken and hurting world.

In the age of #hashtivism, where we are faced with macro and micro problems that seem giant, their voices so amplified, we can easily become like Saul and the Israelites in the story — overwhelmed with fear and inadequacy. This fear can turn our empathy to apathy and our action to atrophy. However, the lesson of David, a king after God's own heart, reminds us that the problems we face, while they might be too big for us, are never too big for God. Using what we have and who we are, with faith in our great God, we can fight the giant problems of our world with hope, and we can find victory.

The problems we face, while they might be too big for us, are never too big for God.

Pursuing God's Heart in a Social Media World

As we approach the horizon of our social media landscape and hear the echoing bravado of the giants that taunt us, may we always remember, like young King David, that although the challenges are big and overwhelming, God is always bigger.

Therefore, as you watch the news channels that trade in "giant-watching," or as you scroll through your social media feeds full of the problems that face your friends and acquaintances, how will you respond? Will you respond like King Saul, in fearful paralysis? Or will you respond like King David, in prayerful and faithful action, believing in a God who is bigger and stronger than all of life's enemies, and asking what role you can play to act out God's will for the world?

Compassion Fatigue

In response to the tsunami of information, problems, and circumstances that social media provides, it is common to experience that feeling of paralysis, of having no more compassion to give. The clinical name for this is *compassion fatigue*. Compassion fatigue is often manifested in institutional care-givers, front-line social workers, and first responders. It affects their professional and personal lives because it alters their view of others. This is a result of an emotional defence-mechanism, but it can cause these front-line workers to develop anxiety, apathy, and cynicism from working with people who have been traumatized and whose needs are great.

This condition is no longer just a problem for those who serve the most beleaguered people in our world; it's become widespread among us. Although social media makes us increasingly aware of problems and enables us to organize and mobilize people like never before to confront and solve these problems, somehow the reverse often happens: instead of motivating people, compassion in such large doses can paralyze people and makes them feel hopeless.

The concept of compassion fatigue can not only help us understand what might be happening to us, it can also provide a helpful framework for working through it. Those who suffer from compassion fatigue are often treated by proper self-care, intentionally focusing on one problem at a time, and deliberately looking at the positives in the world rather than only the challenges. Therefore, I suggest three intentional movements in our lives to break free from our compassion held in captivity: self-care, intentional action, and seeing beauty.

Self-Care

First, it is important to remember self-care. Just as Jesus was regularly moved with compassion to help and heal those in need around him, he also regularly went by himself and spent time with His Father. Jesus knew that rest and retreat were not just a bonus or add-on to life but a necessity for someone who faced the needs of so many people.

Social media has created an age of constant distraction and incessant chatter. Intentionally practicing the spiritual discipline of silence and solitude is foundational to self-care. Just as Jesus regularly went to be alone, so must we. Away from our devices, away from our distractions, and away from outside voices. Time spent alone in silence helps us to tune into the voice of Jesus, the Good Shepherd, who reminds us of God's strength and power, our worth and value, and also our purpose and mission. These moments, when we read God's Word, pray to our Father, and listen for His voice, help to care for our soul, recharge our compassion, and empower us to care for our world with God's compassionate heart and boundless love.

Time spent alone in silence helps us to tune into the voice of Jesus.

If the Son of God intentionally and proactively spent time alone, shouldn't it be important for us, too? May we withdraw and spend time alone with God to be reminded that although the problems of our world are big, our God is bigger.

Intentional Action

Second, as we are faced with giants, the micro and macro challenges of the world, may we look beyond their calls for attention and find one simple step to take. This step will not solve the problem, but it will make some progress towards a solution. Therefore, if you see a friend who is hurting online, post an encouraging comment or message. If there is a natural disaster, do not simply make an expression of social media solidarity, but also some small donation (even if it is only small). When you are tempted to post "thoughts and prayers" and #hashtag a movement in a post, commit to doing something practical to pair with your statement of solidarity. May our actions, however small, be paired with our hashtags.

Although a small donation, simple words, or a letter or phone call to an elected official may seem small, one of the things that social media has taught us is that small actions, networked together, can have a great impact.

When I was in high school, I suffered a traumatic injury to my knee during basketball practice. Thanks to a failed attempt to slam dunk, I broke part of my knee, and the doctors had to screw and staple it back together again. The recovery time was long, and I had to wear a full-length cast for a couple of months, and I missed much of the season. Once the cast was removed and I was finally able to get rid of the horrible residual smell of a plaster cast worn by a teenager for several weeks in the summer, I began the long process of stretching and rebuilding my muscles. With the help of a physiotherapist, I began exercises to increase strength and flexibility. I eventually recovered my full range of motion and strength and could rejoin my team. All physiotherapy starts small and seems to progress slowly. Like physiotherapists for our own souls, we must begin by making small, intentional movements to rebuild and stretch our compassion-muscles.

> **May our actions, however small, be paired with our hashtags.**

As kings and queens entrusted with the democratized power of social media, may we take a lesson from Ben Parker, Spider-Man's uncle: "With great power comes great responsibility." We cannot meet that responsibility with only our intentions, well-wishes, or prayers; we also need our actions. When our prayers and our actions work together, we, like David, have the capacity to defeat the giants before us.

Seeing Beauty

Third, we need to see what God is doing around us instead of only focusing on the challenges that demand our attention. God is always working, and God's beauty is everywhere. We don't naturally notice beauty when we're faced with challenges; we have to train ourselves to pay attention to it. Strange as it might seem, we can learn a lesson from air force pilots in this regard.

Air force pilots are prone to experience a phenomenon known as "G-LOC." This is what happens when they perform tight manoeuvres that increase the gravitational forces — "G-forces" — they experience. These forces cause many symptoms, one of which is tunnel vision. Pilots in the midst of fighting an enemy and employing sharp maneuvers can lose their peripheral vision and become in danger of crashing or inadvertently hitting other aircraft. In our social media world, we experience our own kind of G-LOC: when we are faced too often with our enemy, injustice, we can lose sight of God's beauty even though it's all around us.

Don't get so focused on the problems in our world that you can no longer see all the good things that God is doing and the beauty that surrounds you. This is one of the reasons why the Psalms — the hymns of the Bible, many of which were written by David — are filled with thanksgiving and celebration of the goodness of God. This discipline of thanksgiving and celebration can help to recharge our hope and refocus our perspective.

A Hope-Filled Vision of Compassion in the Age of Kings

When the giants come calling, first pray and ask God what to do, so that you can use all that you are and all that you have, moving in faith toward action and believing the truth that God is bigger than the giants who taunt you. Like David, you may not have the armour of the warrior king, but you have something unique to offer in the fight against the giants of injustice that stand before you. In obedience, and with great courage, use what you have and let God do the rest. There is great freedom in this. There is also rest, focus, and relief from the compassion fatigue that plagues our social media world.

Imagine a world, overwhelmed with social media compassion fatigue, witnessing the Church living compassionately and fighting injustice. Imagine the impact the church could have on the giants of our world if we trusted in God, used what we have, and moved into battle against the giants of our time. The world would stop and pay attention to bold, active, and compassionate faith like that.

In the age of kings and queens, may we not be paralyzed by compassion fatigue when we come face to face with giants. Instead, may prayer be our battle cry and may loving action be our fight against injustice.

A Royal Reflection

Read

- Psalm 118
- This is a psalm of thanksgiving that reminds God's people of God's faithfulness, love, and triumph over enemies. As we consider the injustices before us, may we be reminded of God's goodness, faithfulness, and beauty as we move forward in battle against the injustices in our world.

Reflect

- What giants (micro and macro) are you aware of? What have you seen displayed on your social media feed? List them.
- How have you seen compassion fatigue affect you and your responses to the items on that list?

Respond

- Read Psalm 118 again.
- Spend time alone thanking God. Express thanksgiving for who God is and what God has done.
- Read your list and ask God to show you one giant to focus on. Circle it.
- Ask God what you have that you can use to address the giant you circled.
- What is one practical thing you can do with what you have to move from compassion to action? Write it down and commit to doing it this week.

ACQUAINTANCES

Pinocchio is a complicated character — with a serious conceptual flaw. The wooden puppet with the nose that grows when he lies has a problem, and that problem is a paradox.

What if Pinocchio were to declare, "My nose is growing!"? What would happen? I realize this isn't explored in the classic tale, but imagine it with me.

If his nose grew, the statement would be true, and his nose would be unable to grow. Then, if his nose weren't growing, the statement would be a lie, and it would have to grow. I'm pretty sure Master Geppetto didn't consider Pinocchio's paradox when he carved the wooden boy.

Social media has its own paradox, and, like Master Geppetto, its creators didn't consider the paradox inherent in their creation. One of social media's glaring contradictions is that while social media allows us to be more connected than ever before, it also seems to make people feel more alone and isolated. [8] Sherry Turkle calls this phenomenon "alone together." [9] For the first time in history, people can connect instantly with anyone from anywhere, across multiple devices and — thanks to translation tools — even in multiple languages. But while social media has expanded the breadth of our connections, it has reduced their depth.

I have an average-sized social media relationship circle. Like most people's circles, mine is filled with close friends, close family, and close colleagues, but it also contains high school acquaintances I don't really know anymore, people I've connected with at conferences, celebrities I follow, and members of the different organizations I've been part of. This means that my social media has a broad audience, and that breadth makes depth difficult. How can I publicly share stories about my life in a way that's appropriate for all these different people? I find that I usually do so by aiming for the lowest common denominator. Consequently, I end up sharing the same information with my closest friends that I would be comfortable sharing with my most distant acquaintances. Of course, there are group tools and privacy settings in some social media platforms that could enable me to reserve the more intimate information for those closest to me, but I, like most people I know, don't take the time to set this up originally or manage it consistently.

> **While social media has bestowed upon all of us the royal power of increased connection, it has simultaneously trapped us in our individual throne rooms, isolated by our newly acquired power.**

While social media has bestowed upon all of us the royal power of increased connection, it has simultaneously trapped us in our individual throne rooms, isolated by our newly acquired power. This is the paradoxical relationship that power creates, and people of power have carried the burden of it throughout history. As kings and queens in our age, we have been empowered with both a scepter and a throne. The scepter has expanded our reach, but the throne is narrow and lonely.

The Paradox of the Scepter and the Throne

The royal scepter of social media allows us to connect with more people than ever before. In an instant, wherever I am, I can connect with almost anyone from almost anywhere. All of humanity can be digitally connected. It is tempting and even logical to assume that if we have connection, then we also have community, but that is not true. Community needs connection in order to function, but connection doesn't need community. Hence our social isolation on our narrow thrones.

"Alone together" has been experienced by kings and queens throughout history. As a person gains power, they lose the ability to determine if those close to them really care for them or if they simply want to remain close to the seat of power for their own benefit. For anyone in power, this uncertainty and distrust can be isolating. Consider the response buttons on most social media platforms. These platforms are designed so that followers can respond to a post only with positivity or empathy. If reaction buttons provide only positive reinforcement, then like all kings and queens we are often left not knowing who our true friends are or what they really feel.

The throne also provides some unique powers to kings and queens: the power to choose to engage and disengage with others at will (friending/unfriending and following/unfollowing), the power to silence the voices of friends and foes alike (hiding posts and alerting the algorithms of a preference for what to see or not see), and the power to control who and what other people can see from us (controlled privacy settings). Power like this might be tempting, but it is inherently isolating.

Therefore, it is of little surprise that we are in the midst of a crisis of loneliness, worry, anxiety, and depression in our society. Our culture is readjusting to a new landscape created by the new power of a hyper-relationally-connected world. In this, the media theorist Marshall McLuhan was correct: our emerging age is an age of anxiety. [10]

The Effects of Solitary Confinement

Have you ever imagined what it would be like to be in solitary confinement? Even with access to newspapers, books, or even personal correspondence, the lack of meaningful human interaction can make solitary confinement psychologically devastating. Prisoners who spend time in solitary inevitably end up with deeper psychological wounds than they had when they entered. As one prisoner who spent twenty-four years in solitary confinement remarked, "The worst thing that's ever happened to me in solitary confinement happens every day. It's when I wake up." [11]

One of the dangers of having only relationships that are mediated by social media is that, if we aren't careful, we end up in a digital version of solitary confinement. The effects of solitary confinement on prisoners are disturbingly similar to the characteristics of our social media age: anxiety, depression, hopelessness, mood swings, poor impulse control, and, in some cases, self-harm and suicide. [12]

Because of this, in combination with other cultural factors, our society is, to use the words of the Apostle Paul, groaning as if in the pains of childbirth, longing for redemption (Romans 8:22–24). We are suffering from our isolation and we are longing for true community, relationship, and friendship. We were never created to live in this digital solitary confinement. We have yet to find a way to wield our new-found power of connection and also build and sustain community. This is a skill that we need to master.

The scepter has expanded our reach, but the throne is narrow and lonely.

Kings and queens have always struggled with the way that the breadth of their reach brings loneliness instead of real connection. What does true community and friendship look like for kings and queens like you and me? With the power of our new-found royalty, how do we escape the prisons of our throne rooms and discover true friendship and community?

David's Story Is Our Story

These questions draw us to the story of David and his persistent and enduring friendship with Jonathan. Their unique and loyal relationship demonstrates that friendship is possible for kings and queens. It can also give us specific lessons on how to cultivate true friendship and see it flourish in our social media world.

Learning from the Life of King David
1 Samuel 20

After David defeats Goliath, David is placed in Saul's military service. As David takes on more responsibility as a warrior in the kingdom, his public profile begins to rise, and Saul begins to see David as a threat to his throne.

As the threat grows, David turns to the prophet Samuel in an attempt to confirm his destiny and regain confidence in God's anointing (1 Samuel 19). [13] Having had his identity and destiny confirmed, David runs to his trusted and loyal friend Jonathan (the son of King Saul) for support and assistance. Although David and Jonathan's friendship is an aside in the biblical story, this incident shows that it is an important and beneficial relationship for both of them. Their friendship serves as an example for royals like you and me that friends are vital especially for the role they play in our pursuit of God's calling on our lives. David and Jonathan don't simply show interest in each other's lives; rather, their destinies are interconnected. There is a mutuality in their relationship that goes well beyond pleasantries. Translated to our social media world, they are not simply social media friends who comment on each other's lives from a digital distance; they are trusted and loyal friends who sacrifice, risk, and care for each other.

Loneliness is the pain we feel when we are not living in the kind of community that we were created for.

With the mounting threat of Saul's jealousy, the New Moon festival approaches and David hatches a plan to test Saul's feelings towards him, in a sort of threat-assessment. David instructs Jonathan that if the king notices he is missing at the festival, he should tell the king that David went to Bethlehem to perform the annual sacrifice with his family. If Saul doesn't react in anger, it means David is fine and is safe to return; however, if Saul becomes angry, it means David is in jeopardy. With this simple plan, David and Jonathan reaffirm a mutual covenant (binding commitment) together.

In the original Hebrew, a specific word is used in this story to highlight and define the covenant relationship between David and Jonathan: *hesed*. *Hesed* is used often in the Bible and it typically refers to God's relationship with His people, Israel. The exact meaning of *hesed* (NIV translates it as "kindness" in 1 Samuel 20:8, 14–16) is something of linguistic debate, but it includes a sense of steadfast, faithful, committed, and loving kindness. As 1 Samuel 20:17 states, David loved Jonathan "as he loved himself." David and Jonathan's relationship is one of mutual commitment, with mutual trust and mutual love.

After their relationship is reaffirmed, Jonathan creates a secret signal to communicate to David, who, according to the plan, will be hiding in a field. As the festival commences, Saul notices David's absence, and when Jonathan gives the predetermined excuse to Saul, Saul responds with rage. Saul's rage so engulfs him that he takes it out on Jonathan; threatening David's life and overcome with emotion, Saul throws a spear at his son.

As David suspected, his life is in jeopardy and his exile is about to begin. The following day David and Jonathan secretly reunite in the field, weep together, and recommit their loyalty to each other. David then leaves in exile and Jonathan goes back to town.

I don't think the risk that Jonathan takes or the trust that David puts in Jonathan can be over-emphasized. This is a profound friendship built on an enduring loyalty. David's life is in Jonathan's hands and, as the ensuing story shows, Jonathan's future is David's hands.

I wonder, how many of us have a *hesed*-type friendship like this? How many of us have people for whom we would risk our lives and futures and who would do the same for us? Who do you know who is weeping for you, and who you are weeping for?

Hesed-friendships are a rare experience in our social media world.

Pursuing God's Heart in a Social Media World

The Hope of Community in our Hyper-Connected World

Language evolves and, with it, the phrases we use. I've often wondered if the phrase "That's what friends are for" is at risk of extinction — or at least 'endangered language' status — in our social media age. I wonder if each of us will experience our own version of the scene from the movie *The King's Speech* in which the king's speech therapist says, "That's what friends are for," and King George VI replies, "I wouldn't know."

Is this an emerging cultural refrain?

Does the new power we possess in our social media age make *hesed*-friendships difficult, and the experience of community rare? Although loneliness can afflict anyone, it finds fertile ground in people who hold power.

The paradox of our hyper-connected and yet isolated world creates an ache and longing deep within our souls for something more. Loneliness is the pain we feel when we are not living in the kind of community that we were created for. One need only look at the first pages of the Bible to discover this truth. In it, God creates our world out of nothing, making order out of chaos through the creative act. God then declares, "It is good." This pattern is repeated until the creation of Adam, when God declares that it is not good for Adam to be alone. It is not good for humans to be alone. We have been created with a common desire to know and to be known, to help one another, and to share our experiences. We have been created for friendship, love, and community. This is an essential part of what it means to be human; without it, our hearts ache and we cry out in hunger for community.

We have been created with a common desire to know and to be known, to help one another, and to share our experiences.

Kings and Queens Traveling Alone Together

Watch any royal figure travel and you will see a similar sight: a secured vehicle of some kind, crowds of people gathered to witness the event, and the royal figure waving at a 'safe' distance from the crowd.

Although they are technically in the same physical space as the crowd, the king or queen is distinctly alone, travelling from Point A to Point B. This is an apt image of relationships for our age of kings and queens: each of us travelling alone through life in an individual isolated vehicle (that is, social media profile), waving to each other (with comments, clicks of reactions, or emoticons), and being alone together. But we were created for community, not just connections. We were created for *hesed*-friendships, not just acquaintance.

As I travel through life, I have the priceless, rare gift of a *hesed*-friendship. My Jonathan is named Rob, and he's a fellow pastor and follower of Jesus who knows everything about me just as I know everything about him. We've wept together, laughed together, prayed together, confessed together, challenged each other, and comforted each other. Our relationship has been thoroughly tested over time.

In order to make a *hesed*-friendship grow and flourish, we must lay down the power that kings and queens wield and be truly vulnerable.

Although we live within different cultures and speak with different accents, we have a commonality and a bond that is borderless. I've called Rob at odd hours and unveiled the wounds of my soul over an issue of relational betrayal. I called Rob from the hospital when my youngest son went into open-heart surgery. I distinctly remember sobbing on the phone as Rob prayed for me and my little boy. I've also called Rob to tell him about exciting things that are happening in my church and in my family. I've called Rob countless times to bare my soul just like he's called me to bare his. We talk several times a week and they are always substantive conversations, not because their content is always so significant, but because of the covenant *hesed*-relationship we share.

I share this to affirm that *hesed*-relationships are possible.

I understand that this type of relationship is rare in our age of kings and queens, but it is worth all the gold in the kingdom — and it really is possible. It takes vulnerability, but it is worth the risk. It takes effort, but it is worth the sacrifice. God created you for community; don't give up on pursuing God's design.

Nurturing *Hesed*-Friendships in a World of Acquaintances

As all kings and queens know, power never insulates us from the relational brokenness of our world. All kings and queens feel the pain that comes from relationships gone awry: betrayal, heartbreak, and the sting of lies. At the same time, they know that power often isolates its holder from other people, making real and authentic community more difficult to experience.

It might seem as if we can't grow *hesed*-friendships in a world like ours, but it is still possible to experience the kind of relationships for which we were created. The longing of your heart and the loneliness you experience can be remedied by relationships, but these relationships must be nurtured through prayer, persistence, personal cost, and vulnerability.

As you pursue community in our hyper-connected world, begin with prayer. Ask God to bring a Jonathan into your life. Ask God to give you a *hesed*-friendship to cultivate and grow.

When I was in junior high, I struggled to find a good friend. I had friends, but not a 'best friend.' This broke my mother's heart, and she began to pray for God to give me a friend like that. I know this because I have her hand-written letter tucked into my Bible. I also know that prayer works! God answered her prayer, and I found a wonderful friend who walked alongside me throughout high school. If you are lonely, ask God to show you a friendship that you can cultivate.

As you nurture a *hesed*-friendship, don't give up; be persistent. If you pray and a friend doesn't appear that same day, keep praying. Be persistent in your prayers, but also be persistent when a spark of *hesed*-friendship eventually emerges. Friendships take time to nurture. Like a bonsai tree that takes constant attention and persistent care, and unlike social media connections that happen in an instant, *hesed*-friendships take time. Sometimes, for their roots to grow deeper, they need to endure conflict and difficulty. In a *hesed*-friendship, you will likely have to confront and be confronted, and to forgive and be forgiven. This is part of what makes *hesed*-friendships flourish and grow over time.

I know from my own experience that this is true. My friendship with my friend Rob has withstood times of conflict, disagreement, and disappointment. As Proverbs 27:5–6 says, "Better is open rebuke than hidden love. Wounds from a friend can be trusted, but an enemy multiplies kisses." By leaning in, going deeper, and sticking it out with compassion, patience, and forgiveness, our relationship has strengthened, and the fruit of our relationship has grown sweeter. Therefore, to nurture *hesed*-friendships, don't give up, don't let go, and be persistent.

Hesed-friendships are also costly. We struggle with this in our consumerist culture. However, like all things of great value, friendships cost us; we pay for them with our time and energy. Cultivating friendships will always cost us. In my life, I have paid for travel, spent hours on the phone, spent time helping to build or repair things, and shared countless meals. I have not done any of these by accident and they have created community and relationships that are worth more than all of the investments I have made. Not only has paying this price blessed me with friendships, but it has also given me the opportunity to bless my friends.

Finally, *hesed*-friendships are vulnerable. Social media lets us control what we share and to whom we share it. This is one of its most beloved features. The problem is, *hesed*-friendships are not based on the edited version of ourselves or the edited version of the other person. *Hesed*-friendships are based on the real, broken, and at times unravelled version of ourselves that we pour out in vulnerability before our friends. In order to make a *hesed*-friendship grow and flourish, we must lay down the power that kings and queens wield and be truly vulnerable. Vulnerability is a risk, but, again from my experience, I have been rewarded time and time again for taking the risk. Sure, there are a handful of times when I've been hurt and betrayed in my vulnerability, but those times pale in comparison to the countless opportunities that vulnerability has given me to experience God's gift of community born out of forgiveness, truth, and grace. Take the risk. It is worth it!

> **May we let go of our crowns and grab hold of one another.**

A Hope-Filled Vision of *Hesed*-Friendship in the Age of Kings

Hesed-friendships are rare for kings and queens, but they are possible. As we adjust to the new equilibrium of power that social media has created, may we not give up on the possibility of friendship and community. It is good to be connected, but it is not good to be alone. May your feelings of loneliness show you that God created you for something more, and may the quest for something more drive you into community. That quest for community will demand that you be persistent, pay the cost, and practice vulnerability, all of which are unnatural for royalty. As a culture of people who are groaning in loneliness, may we let go of our crowns and grab hold of one another. *Hesed*-friendships are more than possible; we have been created for them.

What if the church became a community in which we lived as we were designed, in true community with one another? What if, through this community, people truly knew us by our love (John 13:35)? The church, in a social media world desperate for relationship and community, could truly be a city on a hill (Matthew 5:14), a beacon for a lonely world in desperate need of deep relationships and *hesed*-friendship. As we learn to bear the weight of our new power, may we tenaciously pursue community and friendship, and, through our increased connection, invite others to do the same.

A Royal Reflection

Read

- Psalm 59
- Written by David when Saul sent men to David's house to kill him, Psalm 59 is a song and prayer of desperation and a resounding call to God as deliverer.

Reflect

- Where in your life do you feel attacked and alone? What would it mean to trust in God as your deliverer in this situation?
- In the midst of your challenges and difficulties, who do you know whom you can ask for help? Sometimes our times of greatest need are also our greatest opportunities to experience the vulnerability in which *hesed*-friendships flourish.
- Think about the connections in your life. Is there someone who might benefit from your friendship, help, and encouragement? What would it look like to help them today?

Respond

- Pray and ask God to show you the friends you already have with whom you could develop deeper friendships. Also, pray and ask God to give you new relationships that you might cultivate into deep friendships and true community.
- Ask a friend to pray for you in a specific way today. Call or send a text, email, or message, and reach out in vulnerability.
- Ask a friend how you can pray for them in a specific way today. Call or send a text, email, or message, and reach out in encouragement and support.
- Commit to taking a specific and intentional step to deepen a friendship with someone in your life.

TROLLS

When I was in elementary school, my father helped me build the bike of my dreams. Built on the shell of a dirt-bike-style BMX, painted canary yellow, and with a wooden box on the back, it was the physical representation of my creative vision. I loved that bike and couldn't wait to bring it to school and show my friends.

As I pedalled my masterpiece to school on its maiden voyage, I was filled with pride. With a smile of my face, I approached the playground only to be confronted by two schoolyard bullies. From the top of the monkey-bars, they yelled at me, viciously mocking my two-wheeled creation. Whoever said "Sticks and stones may break my bones, but words will never hurt me" didn't know the deep psychological scar-tissue bullying can leave. After thirty years, the words still sting with their venomous bite.

Bullies have always existed. Some were in my schoolyard that day and many more are hiding in the shadows of the internet. With bullies bearing the power of kings and queens, their voices amplified in an anonymous cyber-playground, words have perhaps never been so powerful or painful. And as the Bible teaches, and we will discover, our words have always held the power to bring life or to destroy it.

Amplified Voices in a Levelled Kingdom

If you've ever been to a large political rally or protest, you'll have experienced a small-scale, real-life version of what happens in the social media world. The crowd is diverse, full of people who hold divergent opinions, and they all react differently: some listen intently, others cheer loudly, and some react vitriolically or even violently. According to crowd psychology, as crowd size increases, so does the sense of anonymity, and with it the potential for increased vitriol. In large political rallies and protests it often manifests in verbal outbursts of disrespectful disagreement, swearing, and heckling.

The internet is filled with trolls who make use of its anonymity.

Throughout history, kings and queens have had to face criticism from angry crowds. Now, in the age of social media, the experience has been democratized — given to all. As kings and queens ourselves, we can bear the brunt of vitriol from strangers who dislike and resent us for who we are or for what we've done with our power. Conversely, we now all have the ability to yell anonymously from the crowd and have our voices amplified.

From anonymous accounts in the shadowy corners of social media, you will read cries of outrage, contrasting opinions, hateful rhetoric, and hurtful comments. In a satirical expression of this reality, late-night host Jimmy Kimmel has a segment on his program called Mean Tweets. In this segment, celebrities and politicians read out the mean tweets they've received. This exercise highlights the extreme and irrational vitriol that floods the social media world, but it also attempts to shine light into the shadows and use comedy to take the sting out of the words of those who dwell there.

Trolls

Take a glance in the digital shadows — in any comments section or in replies to tweets — and you will see a gratuitous display of the internet phenomenon known as trolling. Often utilizing provocative language and extreme rhetoric, under the cover of anonymity, trolling is the act of reacting with the intent to provoke.

The term *internet troll* brings to mind two very different images. First, it evokes the image of a fisherman who uses bait on their line and the slow-moving action of a lure pulled behind a boat. Similarly, internet trolls react with charged and provocative language to news stories, posts, pictures, and videos in an attempt to bait people into a fight, elicit a reaction, wound their target, or change an opinion. The second image that trolling evokes is one of the mythical creature who lives in the shadow of a bridge and eats those who attempt to cross. Internet trolls, for their part, live in the anonymity of the digital shadow and attempt to use their words to destroy. They have no desire to listen, reason, or understand. Trolls simply desire to discredit, humiliate, frighten, and otherwise destroy those who cross or disagree with them. The internet is filled with trolls who make use of its anonymity.

Social Media as a Bridge

I have yet to drive across the Confederation Bridge, but I hear it is a marvel to behold. Spanning thirteen kilometers, the bridge drapes the Abegweit Passage of the Northumberland Strait, connecting Prince Edward Island with the mainland (New Brunswick). It is an amazing feat of engineering that currently holds the Guinness World Record for the longest bridge over ice (in winter).

In many ways, this is what social media is for the world: a bridge that connects beyond borders and barriers. It connects everyone everywhere across vast expanses never journeyed before with such ease and speed. The social media age connects everyone and elevates every voice, and it does so seemingly without regard for who is speaking or for what is said.

However, with anonymity thrown into the mix, the power that comes with increased connection and an amplified voice has become both a gift and a curse. As a gift, it allows people to find community and help in situations in which anonymity can enable them to be honest and feel safe. There are many who have found solace and help with their addictions, anxiety, depression, or other challenges thanks to this anonymity.

An early internet phenomenon that demonstrated this is PostSecret.[14] PostSecret is a blog started in 2005 by Frank Warren that publishes homemade postcards of personal secrets that followers of the project mail in anonymously. This social experiment gave a voice to people who felt imprisoned by their secrets, and it exposed many people's sins, desires, and intimate thoughts to the world while keeping those people anonymous. It was embraced as a positive outlet for those who shared their secrets and a source of consolation and support for those who were too timid to share. PostSecret became a place in which people from all over the world could, with the safety of anonymity, reveal their brokenness and begin a healing journey.

The original PostSecret blog didn't contain a comments section, but in the app version comments were allowed. With this change, the anonymity that had once been a blessing and had made the Post-Secret movement possible became a curse. Anonymous commenters trolled and bullied people who had shared the most intimate and even shameful truths about themselves. [15] This illustrates how, although anonymity can be a gift, for some it can also be a curse, because it gives rise to online bullying and trolling.

Complicating matters, corporations and political groups have gamed online anonymity by employing "bots." These artificial social media profiles stir up debate and disagreement by posting content and replies that push a particular agenda. This tactic was used famously in the 2016 presidential election in the United States, and it is still being employed in various forms today. [16] This makes it difficult to discern public opinion, to find out where 'facts' and opinions are coming from, and to wade through the digital noise.

The social media bridge has allowed the world to connect like never before, but it has also provided shelter for the trolls who dwell below.

The social media bridge has allowed the world to connect like never before, but it has also provided shelter for the trolls who dwell below. How do we pursue God's heart in a social media world that gives others the power to troll us, and us the power to troll others?

The Trolls Who Live Under the Bridge

The Norwegian fairy tale of the Three Billy Goats Gruff, adapted for our social media age, has the potential to teach us something about dealing with the kind of trolls we know today. The story begins with three billy goats who need to cross a bridge over a river in order to feed on the delicious fresh grass on the other side.

The smallest billy goat attempts to cross first, and the "trip, trap, trip, trap" of his hooves awakens a troll who had been hiding by the river in the dark shadow below the bridge. Hungry and angry, the troll yells out with a raspy voice, threatening to fight and eat the small young goat. The young goat talks to the troll and convinces the troll to let him go. The troll agrees and sinks back into the shadow to wait.[17]

In the protection of the shadows, we are all tempted to lash out in anger or revenge.

As the first billy goat makes it to the green pastures on the other side of the bridge, the second billy goat enters with the familiar sound, "trip, trap, trip, trap." The troll is awakened again and, his hunger even greater than before, threatens to eat the goat. The second goat responds in the same way as the first, convincing the troll to let him go and, once again, the troll sinks back into the shadow and waits.

Finally, the third billy goat arrives and the troll viciously attacks. But this time, the third goat is bigger than the second and much bigger than the first. Unphased by the troll, the large billy goat lowers his head and pushes the troll into the water below. Now free to cross the bridge at will, the goats graze on either side of the bridge.

And the troll? The troll has been brought into the light, has been cleansed by the water, and has rediscovered his true identity: a once lonely and angry goat who had been living in the shadows for too long (yes, I've editorialized the ending a bit!).

Billy Goat Lessons on Dealing with Trolls

This classic tale is usually interpreted as a story about waiting until we have gathered the resources, created the alliances, or completed the training to confront a problem that faces us. Although this is the obvious interpretation for the original form of the tale, I want to suggest that we view this story through a new lens that makes it more relevant for our time.

First, this fairy tale has much to teach us about the nature of trolls. It reminds us that trolls exist and thrive in the shadows. The troll is not sitting on the bridge for all to see and enjoying the sunlight. Rather, the troll is hiding below in the secrecy and anonymity that darkness provides. We often react differently when no one is watching us; when alone, we do and say things we would never do and say if we were in public and could be held accountable for our words and actions.[18]

This tale also reminds us that we don't have to fight every battle we face. Social media is filled with an endless parade of people who want to pick a fight. Like the first two goats, sometimes we don't have to engage in the fight and can keep walking. As the old saying goes, you don't have to show up for every argument you are invited to. Some battles aren't worth fighting.

Trolls exist and thrive in the shadows.

However, sometimes we are the third billy goat, and it *is*

up to us to fight the battle. When that's the case, it doesn't mean that we have to fight using the weapons and tactics of a troll; rather, we should fight with the best weapons available to us in God's kingdom of light: truth, kindness, and love.

Finally, what if we are the troll? Maybe my alternative ending can give us hope. If the troll in the story is just a goat who has been alone and in the shadows for too long, this means that we have the choice to be the goat or to be the troll. If a troll can be invited into the light and cleansed in the water, that means that hope for the troll — hope that they might reclaim their true identity — is also worth fighting for.

It is easy to demonize internet trolls, seeing them as a small number of strangers, but, statistically, if you have used the internet, there is a high likelihood that you have commented on something or written something negative about someone else, displaying troll-like characteristics in anonymous forums. A Pew Research poll found that 41% of Americans have been harassed online.[19] With a victim list this alarming, there must be a perpetrator list just as shocking. We are more like trolls than we would like to admit, but there is hope that we can reclaim our true identity again.

David's Story Is Our Story

The story of David contains an interesting parallel to this. On the run from King Saul, David ends up in the position of a troll, in the shadow of a cave, tempted by the opportunity to kill Saul. If David kills God's anointed King of Israel, he will secure his own safety and have the chance to claim the throne in his own time. What does he choose to do? And, as kings and queens in our social media world, when faced with opportunities to attack in the shadows, what will we choose to do?

Learning from the Life of King David
1 Samuel 24

David's story continues to unfold in the desert, on the run from King Saul who is actively trying to hunt down and kill David, whom Saul perceives as a threat to his throne. While David hides with his gathered men in the desert near En Gedi, King Saul takes three thousand men to pursue David in an act of blood-thirsty self-protection.

In a scene out of a comedic spy novel, King Saul, while in pursuit, goes into a cave to relieve himself. Unbeknownst to Saul, David happens to be hiding in that very cave with his men. Seeing his opportunity to grasp power and take revenge, David reaches out from the darkness. He cuts off a portion of Saul's regal robe, but he stops himself short of killing him.

There are a couple of things to take note of here. First, there are two people in the shadows, but they are there for different purposes: Saul is in the shadows in a state of physical vulnerability looking for privacy, while David is hiding for protection — at least at first. Once an opportunity arises for David, he makes a disrespectful act against the king. **Don't feed the trolls! It's not worth arguing with someone who is not willing to listen.** David uses the shadow not for protection anymore but rather for the opportunity to attack Saul and steal Saul's power for himself, all while Saul is vulnerable but thinks he is safe.

Although David doesn't give in to the temptation to kill Saul, what he does is still an act of symbolic rebellion and disregard for Saul's throne.

David immediately feels his conscience rebuke him for betraying and dishonouring the king: "The Lord forbid that I should do such a thing to my master, the Lord's anointed, or lay my hand on him; for he is the anointed of the Lord" (1 Samuel 24:6). Deeply disturbed by his own actions and wishing to repent, David then risks his safety and steps out of the dark cave into the light, where he asks for King Saul's forgiveness. Saul accepts David's apology and they both go on their way.

Anonymity rarely breeds healthy critique, but critique that comes from within a trusted community can be life-giving.

What makes David's actions even more remarkable and applicable is that in many ways David would have been justified in taking revenge and lashing out against Saul. Saul has tried to kill David repeatedly and Saul has abandoned his commitment to God. David repents not because Saul is innocent or worthy of the throne but because David is committed to God and knows that his anointing by God is subject to God's timing. As we face trolls online, our lashing out in revenge can be equally problematic.

In the protection of the shadows, we are all tempted to lash out in anger or revenge. Like all people of power, we are tempted to either protect the power we have or take it from others. David had the perfect opportunity to seize the throne for himself, but although he symbolically dishonoured Saul's power, he stopped short of taking it completely. As men and women in the new age of kings and queens, how will we respond to others when we are in the shadows? Will we lash out in anger, self-protection, or revenge, or will we control ourselves, repent of our harmful actions, and treat all people as God's beloved?

Pursuing God's Heart in a Social Media World

Social media has given us a bridge that connects us like never before and has the potential to empower everyone. The challenge for kings and queens who live in this new reality is to use this bridge in a way that honours both our own power and the power of others. We, like the billy goats gruff in the reframed fable, walk across the bridge with a trip and a trap. How will we respond to the trolls who attack from the shadows?

The Trip

Trolls love to trip us on the social media bridge. As we walk across the bridge, the trolls will try to convince us that the lies they tell us about ourselves are true. We might be tempted to believe their rhetoric of hate, which will slowly chip away at our self-esteem and identity. As Proverbs 15:4 says, "The soothing tongue is a tree of life, but a perverse tongue crushes the spirit." As they attempt to trip us, may we remember three truths about trolls and how to protect against them.

Trolls love people who travel alone. When you are faced with a troll, don't face them alone — face them in community.

Surround yourself with friends who will support you, remind you of your worth and value, and keep you grounded in the truth of who you are in Jesus. Remember, trolls love to strike people online for two reasons: they are anonymous and they assume we are alone. Community can give us security by reminding us of our value and worth.

Trolls love to be fed. Don't feed the trolls! It's not worth arguing with someone who is not willing to listen. Do your best to let it go and move on. Remember, trolls aim to entice a reaction and escalate the situation, so do your best to respond with love, kindness, and grace. As 1 Peter 3: 9 says, "Do not repay evil with evil or insult with insult. On the contrary, repay evil with blessing, because to this you were called so that you may inherit a blessing."

Trolls love anonymity. Confrontation is an important part of relationships and life. As we will discover in a future chapter, it is something we need to embrace, but we should do so in the right context. Anonymity rarely breeds healthy critique, but critique that comes from within a trusted community can be life-giving. A few years ago, a friend privately messaged me about a poorly phrased social media post I wrote. It was hard to hear but I appreciated the critique and learned an important lesson, and our relationship grew in trust as a result. Feedback is good, but vitriolic critique from an anonymous troll is not worth listening to.

May we consider carefully how we wield this power in our age, and use our new-found royal power to bring life and healing to our world.

Trolls are waiting to trip us in their lies and hate. Don't fall for their deceptive arguments and falsehoods; either ignore them completely or respond with blessing, love, and kindness. You can't try to beat a troll by becoming a troll, because if you do, you end up tripping into their trap.

The Trap

As we walk across the social media bridge, the trolls will also try to trap us into becoming trolls ourselves. In response, we can mimic the trolls' tactics and end up in the shadows with them. When we are tempted into the shadows, it is important to remember that our words have the power either to breathe life or to breathe death. The Book of James reminds us of this: "the tongue is a small part of the body, but it makes great boasts. Consider what a great forest is set on fire by a small spark" (James 3:5). Likewise, Proverbs 12:18 declares, "The words of the reckless pierce like swords, but the tongue of the wise brings healing."

Just as David caught himself in the darkness of a cave with the temptation to strike Saul, so we can be caught with the temptation to lash out at someone with vitriol and hatred, tempted to either protect the power we have or take it from someone else. It would be dangerous to underestimate the power of our words at a time when they are so amplified. Instead, may we consider carefully how we wield this power in our age, and use our new-found royal power to bring life and healing to our world.

A Hope-Filled Vision of Life-Giving Words in the Age of Kings

Just as David found life and hope in the light outside the cave, there is hope for kings and queens like you and me. Whether you are a victim of a troll or a troll yourself, there is hope. Although social media is known for how it amplifies negative voices, it is important to remember that it holds the same power to magnify Jesus as "the way, the truth, and the life." (John 14:6) Imagine the impact on the social media landscape if Jesus-followers leveraged the megaphone of social media for the Kingdom of God. Imagine the church using words to bring life in a world that is desperately crying out for it.

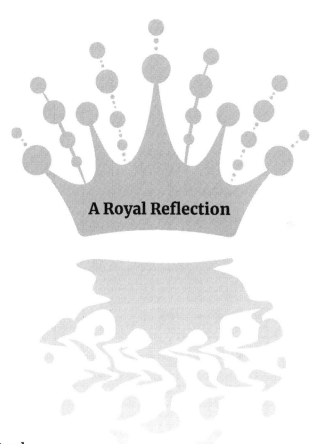

A Royal Reflection

Read

- Psalm 57: This psalm was written by David when he fled from Saul and was hiding in the desert cave.

Reflect

- Have you ever been bullied online? What was it like? How did it make you feel?
- Have you ever bullied someone online? Why did you do it? How do you think it made the other person feel?

- How might online bullying be connected with the pursuit of power?

Respond

- This week, seek three intentional opportunities to use your online words to build life into someone else.
- This week, look for ways to confront injustice, hatred, or falsehood with love, grace, and truth. Find a troll and show them love.
- Pray that God would soften your heart, make you increasingly aware of the power of your words on social media, and use you to build His kingdom.

SELFIES

One of the most dreaded days in junior high is picture day. Hundreds of pubescent, self-conscious, and deodorant-deprived pre-teens prepare for the moment when their awkwardness will be captured for the ages. The students line up like convicts in a prison line awaiting their time in the photographic torture-chair.

In my experience in the late eighties, as the students approached the photographer the backdrops were revealed: faded bookshelves (for the appearance of intelligence) and multi-coloured lasers and florescent paint streaks (to enshrine the modernity of the late eighties and early nineties). Picture day, ironically, never ended with a smile. Instead, it was remembered as a day of forced smiles and faded backdrops of lies.

My cynicism and bitterness aside, junior high picture day is a fitting metaphor for our social media, selfie-driven world. Instead of a faded canvas backdrop, we have our world itself, with its moments and memories, and we have each stepped further into the foreground of our existence. In our selfie age, we are tempted to move ourselves to the centre of our story and view the world as nothing more than a backdrop to our lives.

The Selfie

I have a theory about the inception of the selfie: I think it was first conceived by a far-sighted, technologically-naive senior trying to read a meme on their grandchild's smartphone. In an effort to read the small text, they extended their arm as far out as possible only to accidently take a picture of themselves.

Wherever the selfie originated, there is no doubt that it's become ubiquitous. There are even countless accessories to make them easier. Selfie sticks to mini-drones show us that selfies are here to stay. The ubiquitous selfie is a reflection of social media culture that has, in its unequipped immaturity, fostered a perspective that centres on the self.

In our selfie age, we are tempted to move ourselves to the centre of our story and view the world as nothing more than a backdrop to our lives.

A selfie is a selfie not because the picture includes us but because we are both photographer and subject, which makes everything else (our friends, the scenery, the moment, or the memory) simply the background. In a selfie, we are both the proclaimed and proclaimer. We are both the story and storyteller. We are both celebrity and paparazzo.

If you talk to any funeral director, they'll have a story of people taking selfies at funerals. I've heard stories of people taking selfies at funeral viewings, with the mourner as subject and the deceased as backdrop. Similarly, if you talk to any wedding officiant, they will tell you stories of people, including members of the wedding party, taking selfies with the bride and groom as backdrop — sometimes during the ceremony itself. Moments of remembrance and celebration have been reduced to the backdrop of our lives, shared on social media and projected to the world.

Let me be clear: selfies are not sinful, but self-centredness is. A selfie can be an innocuously convenient way to take a picture, but it also provides a gateway to focus on oneself as the centre of one's story and existence. Like all technology, the selfie is simply a means of extending our reach, and selfies have the unique capacity to help us grab hold of what is already easiest for us: self-centredness.

Selfies are taken by almost everyone, almost everywhere, and they have successfully mixed and amplified two defining characteristics of contemporary North American culture: individualism and celebrity.

A Selfie-Centric Cocktail

Together, the social media age and the selfie have unintentionally mixed a cocktail of individualism and celebrity. Selfie-culture gives us the ability to focus on ourselves to the point that we can each become the centre of our every story. We live this way, we post this way on social media, and, increasingly, we even interpret Scripture this way — often without realizing it.

How often have you heard someone read a verse and then explain what it means "to them"? This subjective and individualistic interpretive approach can be very misleading.

Often, it means that the interpreter decides what the text is saying based on what they would like it to say.

Specifically, consider the Spiritual Gift movement in the church. In teaching on spiritual gifts that I hear and read, more often than not these gifts are interpreted through an individualistic lens. I've heard statements like, "God has given each of us spiritual gifts and our job is to figure out what they are, so we can use them and experience the most joy and fulfillment possible. If you are not experiencing joy and satisfaction as you serve in the church, you are not using your gifts." This sounds good to an ear that's tuned to individualism. However, spiritual gifts are not given by God to the individual for the primary purpose of the individual's personal fulfillment; they are given to the church, as a community, for the purposes of the church. They are entrusted to the individual for the sake of the body, so that all parts may serve together in God's mission.

In a selfie, we are both the proclaimed and proclaimer. We are both the story and storyteller. We are both celebrity and paparazzo.

Additionally, consider how we — at least we evangelicals — share the Gospel. Too often the Gospel message is distilled down to the idea of asking Jesus into our hearts and lives. This subtle phraseology reeks of individualism. It falsely assumes that each of us is the centre of our own story and existence, and that God joins us. The truth is that Jesus does not join our mission, our purpose, or our plan; we join His. The truth is that Jesus invites us into His life and His story. Abundant and eternal life is not found in Jesus entering your life but in you entering His. Abundant life is not found in making your life better but in losing your life and finding His (Matthew 10:39).

These examples illustrate how prevalent individualism is in our culture. We have taken others, and even God, out of the centre of our stories and placed ourselves there as the hero. Individualism is so dominant that it influences how we see, hear, and understand things without us even noticing it. Selfies did not create this reality (it has always existed to some degree), but through the vehicle of the selfie this reality is propelled forward. The selfie shapes how we tell our stories and interpret the world.

The other ingredient in the selfie-centric cocktail is the fascination with celebrity. One of the democratizing effects of social media is that it allows anyone to become a pseudo-celebrity in a celebrity-centric culture. Social media has given everyone everything they need to reach everyone else, and with that comes the possibility of fame. Blogging sites enable anyone to be an author, video sharing sites enable anyone to broadcast their opinion, music-sharing sites enable anyone to be a professional musician, and live-streaming enables anyone to have their own live television show.

Humans were never intended to carry fame and glory. Consequently, it is so much easier than it ever has been to see ourselves as the stars of our own stories, and to act on that perception. For many, the pursuit of online celebrity has become an obsession or even an addiction, because it's so easy to over-indulge in the selfie-centric cocktail.

The problem with seeking celebrity, fame, and glory is not the glory itself but rather who we ascribe it to. In selfie-centrism, glory and fame are all about *us*. But humans were never intended to carry fame and glory. Rather, we were created to give glory and worship to God and to God alone. Glory is a burden we were not intended to bear, and when we try to carry it we become overwhelmed with fear.

David's Story Is Our Story

This reality is experienced in the life of King David and what I'm tempted to call the first red carpet event. At this point in his story, David is a new king who has the praise of his people and the affection of his kingdom. He seeks to bring the Ark of the Covenant back to Jerusalem and discovers the need to direct all glory to God. As the Ark enters Jerusalem, David worships with abandon. True freedom is found in true worship, and true worship means giving all glory to God.

Learning from the Life of King David
2 Samuel 6

As we pick up the story of David, we find him newly crowned king. After winning the battle against the Philistines and the conquering Jerusalem, King David decides it's time to bring the Ark of the Covenant, which holds the Ten Commandments and represents God's presence and glory, to Jerusalem, the City of David (2 Samuel 5:9).

This is a strategic decision. The Ark of the Covenant has both symbolism and power. Moving the Ark to Jerusalem signifies that the power of the presence of God is at the centre of David's reign. With victorious momentum, David orders that the Ark be moved from Bahaal to Jerusalem. Although this decision is strategic, it is also made in haste, and the lack of detailed preparations and ritual care in moving the holy object lead to disastrous consequence. The Ark is carried on a cart, and the oxen moving the cart slip. In an attempt to steady the Ark, Uzziah touches it. God strikes Uzziah dead. Chronicles 15 explains that God did so because David and the Israel-ites did not follow God's commands about how the Ark was to be carried and moved. Although it might seem like an over-reaction by an angry God, it is rather David and the Israelites' under-reaction to the awesomeness, holiness, and reverence of God that is to blame. God gave them specific instructions on how to move and treat the Ark and, in their haste, they ignored them.

God is glorious, and the powerful who recognize it will dance in the freedom it brings.

As a result, the Ark is placed in Obed-Edom's house for three months. After that time, David returns there to make the seven-mile journey to Jerusalem. David, in a desire to honour the glory and holiness of God, sacrifices a bull and a calf for every six steps he takes. Although the action might seem barbaric and foreign to us, at the time the blood sac-rifice acknowledged the sin of the people and the holiness of God; it is a visual sign of God's unsurpassed glory and hol-iness. Consequently, the road between Obed-Edom's house to the City of David (Jerusalem) would have been stained red by blood.

Upon entering Jerusalem, David dances with all his might, lifting his garment in an act of unreserved worship. This inaugural red-carpet event acknowledges the glory of God that even the most powerful among us should recognize. God is glorious, and the powerful who recognize it will dance in the freedom it brings.

Pursuing God's Heart in a Social Media World

Do you know where the Hollywood tradition of the red carpet comes from? Although no one knows for sure, some point to the fact that red dyes were known to be the most expensive and, thus, only used for those of great importance and power. Some point to ancient Greece and the play Agamemnon when the king's wife used a red carpet to welcome home her husband from the Trojan war (her husband refused to walk on it because he was a man and not a god). Some point to the early 1900s and the plush red carpet in the luxurious cars of the New York Central Railroad. Interestingly, it wasn't until the 1920s that the red carpet was used by Hollywood to signify the new royalty in America: movie stars and celebrities. [20]

We were never intended to hold the glory of the crown, the power of popularity, and the victory of the battle.

What if the origin of the red carpet goes back even further? What if the red carpet tradition originated the moment David set out on his seven-mile journey with the Ark of the Covenant and stained the road with blood to signify and celebrate the holiness and glory of the one true God? What if it originated to remind King David (and the Israelites) that he was not the hero of Israel, but God was? This striking event reminded everyone who witnessed it that the glory did not belong in the hands of David, but in God and God alone.

As David experiences in this narrative, releasing the glory that belongs only to God is a freeing exercise. We were never intended to hold the glory of the crown, the power of popularity, and the victory of the battle. Thus, like David, when we do try to seek and hold glory, we break under its weight. Therefore, when we acknowledge that glory can only be held by God and the weight is lifted, we have only one response: worship, which makes us truly free.

Conversely, grasping at glory creates fear. When we seek glory and fame for ourselves, we fear that we will never get it, and if we do get it, we fear we will lose it. Glory, fear, and freedom are intricately connected. If we seek and try to keep glory, we will be bound by fear, but if we offer all glory to God in worship, we will live in freedom. Two fears prevalent in our social media word are the Fear of Missing Out (FOMO) and the Fear of Being Ignored (FOBI).

Fear of Missing Out (FOMO)

Social media selfie-culture can play on and increase our fear of missing out on things. As we look at our social media feeds full of selfies of other people's experiences and real-time reactions to them, it can instill in us a fear that we are missing something important or amazing. This fear can make us feel regret, anxiety, and depression, leading people to spend their time and money on experiences or products they would otherwise be ignorant of.

Any cursory internet search for "FOMO" will provide countless sites teaching various techniques to leverage FOMO to sell and market products and services, using phrases like,

"Have you joined our exclusive get fit club?" or "Don't miss what everyone will be talking about." FOMO feeds on the fears of social media users.

Fear of Being Ignored (FOBI)

Empty soup cans make excellent microphones and horrible headphones. When I was a kid we would use the world's worst communication technology: two empty soup cans and a piece of string. Stringing the cans together, we would try to use the gizmo as a walkie-talkie. Like with most technologies, the fantasy of what it could accomplish was better than the reality. Social media does something similar.

Social media, in its infancy, has made excellent talkers and horrible listeners. This reality has led to *athazagoraphobia*. Athazagoraphobia is the fear of being ignored or forgotten. With social media's ability to see and connect everyone everywhere, we can begin to fear that people are not listening or looking at what we post.

There have been countless times when people on my social media feed have expressed this fear. These people express great concern (often hidden in a complaint about changing algorithms) when people don't like, comment, or share their posts. This isn't by accident. Studies have suggested that we have a neurological response to the positive reactions we receive online. [21] Once we begin to taste the allure of celebrity (expressed psychologically and even chemically in our brains), it is hard to step away from it. Once we've been centre-stage it is hard to go back to the audience.

Living in Freedom

In a selfie-centric culture that views memories and people as backdrops to an individual person's story, we can be held captive by our own storylines. If the plotlines we write always use us as the hero at the centre of our story, we are placing ourselves in an unsustainable and even idolatrous situation. We will be crushed under the weight of it and the fear it can produce. We were never created to be the centre of our stories. When we attempt this, we end up bound by fear — fear of missing out on something, of being ignored, or of failing. The selfie-centric story will always end poorly.

Once we've been centre-stage it is hard to go back to the audience.

However, there is a better story!

This better story has a very different storyline with a very different hero. This hero never fails or forsakes. By reframing our lives under this new story, we can find freedom. Just as King David found freedom in worshipping and giving all the glory to God as the hero and protector of Israel, so can we as we place Jesus at the centre of our story.

Freedom comes when we focus on Jesus rather than on ourselves. Freedom comes when we worship the one to whom all glory belongs. Freedom comes, even when adversity surfaces, because, as Hebrews 12:1b-2a says, we can "run with perseverance the race marked out for us, fixing our eyes on Jesus, the pioneer and perfecter of faith."

Dancing in God's Perspective

In my high school gym class, we covered a variety of sports.

Rather surprising to me at the time, one of the sports we covered was ballroom dance. We learned square-dancing, the waltz, the tango, and even the two-step.

The dance unit was even worse than picture day! Imagine thirty awkward, uncoordinated, shy, and terrified teenagers each matched with a person of the opposite sex, embarrassingly dancing together out of rhythm. The collective undeodorized sweat glands created quite the stench. There were awkward laughs, sore feet from missteps, and many a bruised ego. It was horrendous!

Freedom comes when we focus on Jesus rather than on ourselves.

Although we hated every second of it, unlike algebra it actually proved useful in adult life on several occasions. I have waltzed and done the two-step at many weddings and celebrations.

I would like to propose a *social media two-step* that can help us dance our way out of the cultural pull towards a selfie-centric perspective. The two-step I would like us to learn has God as the lead partner and comprises two specific movements.

Move to the *top*. Get some perspective. Spend time recounting your story from God's perspective. In many ways, we see David do this in the Psalms as he tells the story of Israel from God's perspective, with God as Israel's hero. This perspective breaks down the fears that grow within us when we try to carry the glory that belongs to God. Spend time journaling and praying through your story from God's perspective and see how God has been working His storyline in and through you. Begin to see your life from God's perspective, and freedom will begin to replace fear.

Move to the *side.* Take time and encourage a friend. Bear witness for them. Help them see God at work in their life as the hero of their story. God is a hero who is also faithful and true to God's character and promises. By helping someone else, two things will also happen. First, you will be forced out of a self-centred perspective and you will begin to see how God is working in the lives of people around you. Second, you will begin to grasp a renewed vision of God's work in your own life. We can often see God's work in the lives of others more clearly than we can see it in our own. Begin to see others' lives from God's perspective and your vision for God at the centre of your life will begin to grow, and, again, freedom will begin to replace fear.

We can often see God's work in the lives of others more clearly than we can see it in our own.

These two movements of the *social media two-step* will lead you to trust in God as your leader in the dance of your life. And that kind of trust brings joy.

What story are you living in? Are you at the centre of your story, or is Jesus? Fear exists when we are at the centre, but freedom reigns when Jesus is.

In our social media age, in which stories and images abound, may we live in and tell the Jesus story through the power we have been given as kings and queens. May we reframe the selfie movement and put Jesus back in the centre of our lives. May we seek Jesus' glory and fame, celebrating what He is doing in the lives of others and the world around us. There is a story to tell and the story is Jesus.

A Hope-Filled Vision of God's Glory in the Age of Kings

There was hope for King David even when he forgot the importance of giving God all the glory. As we place Jesus at the centre of our lives and reframe our lives around Him, we will find freedom and hope in a world that is being crushed under the weight of fear.

Imagine the power of the church, equipped to use social media as a listening device to hear what God is doing in the world and sharing God's story through its megaphone. Imagine the impact it would have for a culture bound in fear at the centre of its own story to see the Church living in freedom by centring on God's story and pursuing God's glory.

Just as the development of a child begins with a self-centred view and eventually develops over time to show increasing care towards others, there is hope for social media users to develop in the same way. With the technological advancement of social media, the potential to tell God's story in the world has never been so great. As we mature in our use of it, may we leverage it to share a better story, the Jesus story, and find freedom as we do.

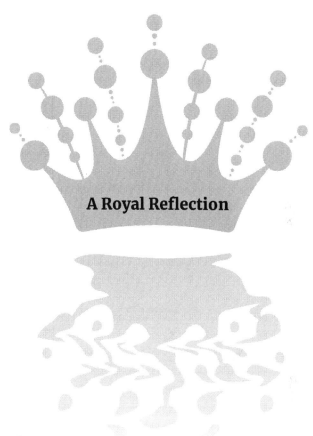

A Royal Reflection

Read
- Psalm 30
- This psalm was written by David for the dedication of the temple.

Reflect
- How might you be affected by FOMO or FOBI?
- In a selfie-centric social media culture, we get focused on social media as a megaphone, but what if we used it to

listen? As you use social media today, listen to what people are posting and ask yourself the following questions:
- What is God doing in the world?
- What is God doing in those around you?
- Use what you have learned to pray.

Respond
- Use Psalm 30 as a prayer of worship and give glory to God.
- Use what you learned from listening to your social media feeds to pray for others and for God's work in the world.

DESIRE

I was a young adult when the internet became a common utility. I can still hear the hum of my 14.4 KBPS modem connecting to the internet.[22] For the first time in my life, I had instant access to encyclopedias, websites, message boards, email, and gaming sites — and pornography. As fast as the internet spread, pornography on the internet spread faster.

As a teen, I never really struggled with pornography. I stumbled across it a few times, but I never really sought it out. But, the first week that we had internet service, my curiosity got the better of me. After a week or two of searching it online, I confessed this to a mentor and made a course-correction in my life. But since then, it has always been a possibility, just a click or tap away.

I share this to identify a reality of our digital social media age. The internet has made pornography a common part of people's experience. I'm not saying it's good or acceptable, but it's a struggle typical of people of all ages, genders, and religious backgrounds. Pornography is an equal-opportunity temptation and, with the power and reach of information technology and social media, it knows no bounds.

The Mobiquity of Pornography and Illicit Online Relationships

Several years ago, I conceived the term *mobiquity* in an analysis that I wrote about Google Glass; I combined the words *mobility* and *ubiquity* to express the ubiquity of mobile devices.[23] The word expresses a reality of our mobile digital age: that seemingly endless information and images are at our beck and call at any given moment. This means that not only are our devices *mobiquitous*, but our tempters are, too. The objects of our desire might be only a click or swipe away, and simply knowing that fact can increase our desire for them.

Because of this, one of the characteristics of the Age of Kings is that it's an age of desire. Consider the following statistics:

- One in every thousand tweets is pornographic.[24]
- Social networks are regularly used by bots to drive traffic to pornographic sites.[25]
- 47% of Christians say pornography is a major problem in the home.[26]
- According to Covenant Eyes (online accountability software):
  - 1 in 5 mobile searches is for pornography.
  - 24% of smartphone owners admit to having pornographic material on their mobile handset.
  - 51% of male and 32% of female students first

viewed porn before their teenage years (12 and younger).

- 66.5% of young men and 48.7% of young women say viewing porn is an acceptable way to express one's sexuality. [27]

Although the veracity of these statistics might be up for debate, on an anecdotal level, even a cursory examination of the internet and social media can show that pornography not only exists online, it thrives there. The same thing can be said of illicit online relationships. Sites like Ashley Madison are designed to help people have extramarital affairs. They are *mobiquitous*, and their presence is still growing.

Pornography is an equal-opportunity temptation and, with the power and reach of information technology and social media, it knows no bounds.

In a matter of twenty years, our society has changed radically. In the same way that I can now access Netflix on my phone rather than having to go to my local Blockbuster, I can now also access pornography on my phone without having to go to the local adult video store. Additionally, I can now access illicit relationships through social networks and online communities with relative anonymity. Consequently, pornography and illicit online relationships have become a social epidemic that thrives in the darkness, and it can shackle people with shame and guilt.

Social media, alongside the endless supply of information on the internet that can be accessed anonymously, has given the power of kings and queens to everyone. In the same way that royalty could command that their sexual desires be met, we command an enormous database of resources that exist to both fulfil and fuel our desires, and it's only ever a click away. We have not been equipped to deal with that power. The challenges that kings and queens had with their sexual power have become challenges for all of us.

David's Story Is Our Story

Sexual acts are not always about desire; they can also be about power. This is the case with rape, sexual misconduct, sexual harassment, and sexual abuse. Kings and queens throughout history have certainly exerted their power to fulfill their sexual desires, but they have also used sex to exert their power.

This exertion of power to fulfill one's sexual desire is seen specifically in the life of King David and his adulterous relationship with Bathsheba. As kings and queens in our social media world, we have much to learn from King David's sexual sin and subsequent actions.

Learning from the Life of King David
2 Samuel 11

When people retell the narrative of David's life, there are two stories that get the majority of the attention. The first is the story of David and Goliath, which gives an image of a triumphant and faith-filled David who moves into battle, in contrast to Saul, who was paralyzed by fear. The other is the story of David and Bathsheba, the story of King David using his power to take advantage of a woman and then abusing his power further by having her husband killed to cover up his transgression. The first story exemplifies the virtues of David, while the second exemplifies his vices.

The story of David and Bathsheba is a fascinating case study with direct application in our digital age. The story begins like many a story of sexual sin: with boredom. Verse one begins, "In the spring, at the time when kings go off to war, David sent Joab out with the king's men and the whole Israelite army. They destroyed the Ammonites and besieged Rabbah. But David remained in Jerusalem." David is supposed to be with his army at war, but instead he is home in Jerusalem and alone with his boredom. One evening, David begins to wander and ends up on his rooftop. From that vantage point, he sees a beautiful woman bathing.

The challenges that kings and queens had with their sexual power have become challenges for all of us.

Note that even though he has many women at his disposal, David still desires more. The desire to see one more image or have one more sexual experience is not new to our social media world; it has always been around, and people of power have had a unique ability to pursue that desire.

David finds out who the woman is, and that she's married to Uriah, one of David's loyal soldiers. That doesn't deter David. Rather, David leverages his power to have her brought to him, and he has sex with her. This is not Bathsheba's initiative. David is the instigator here. David is the one at the centre of power, and he abuses that power to have sex with a woman who is married to someone else. [28] Note that there is no mention of relationship, affection, or love between

David and Bathsheba — just David's bare lust wielded by his powerful hands.

As the story unfolds, we discover that Bathsheba has become pregnant. Now David has a problem: he might be caught in his sin, so he begins to make excuses and covers his tracks. David calls Uriah home from battle under false pretenses, hoping to get Uriah to sleep with Bathsheba so that Uriah (and everyone else) will believe that he is the father of the child. What David doesn't count on is Uriah's honour and solidarity with his fellow soldiers. Unlike David, who seems to be ignoring the battle going on, Uriah refuses to go inside to sleep with his wife while his comrades at arms are still at war.

Failing to cover up his sin as planned, David sends Uriah back to battle, and with him he sends secret orders telling Joab to send Uriah to the front lines and abandon him so that he will die. In this murder by proxy, David loses many men (including Uriah), all to cover up his sin. After Uriah's death, Bathsheba grieves her husband's death and David takes her as his wife.

Pursuing God's Heart in a Social Media World

David's sexual misconduct is the quintessential sexual sin of a person in power: David desires, demands, and gratifies. This reality is now democratized, and the pattern of David in this account is a familiar pattern for people who hold power and have the temptation of lust. The first step in counselling people of power is to help them acknowledge their propensity to this behaviour and then to help them recognize its predictable pattern.

Since the fall, lust has always been a struggle for humans, but the power that social media and the internet have given us has amplified this struggle in the same way it was amplified for kings and queens of old. Consequently, this chapter is not for someone else; it is for you. We are all tempted to fall into this pattern, and we all have ample opportunity to give in to that temptation. Therefore, I invite you to begin by humbly acknowledging that we are all sexual beings, and that information technology and social media have amplified our potential to explore our sexual brokenness, allowing us to gaze further and extend our lustful reach.

The Familiar Pattern of Desire

Like King David, we have a propensity to boredom. David's boredom drew him up onto his roof, while ours takes us to our devices: surfing and scrolling. This is how it often begins for the countless people I have counselled who are tempted with pornography or online relationship sites. Whether it hits us during the tedium of a monotonous job, while we're waiting for an appointment, or when we're killing time before bed, our boredom breeds temptation.

David's pattern of desire unfolds when he sees a beautiful woman bathing. David, in its own moral quagmire, has a harem of women to choose from, and yet this

Information technology and social media have amplified our potential to explore our sexual brokenness, allowing us to gaze further and extend our lustful reach.

married woman catches his attention. This is a reminder that when it comes to lust, enough is never enough. There is always one more video to watch and one more image to view. Lust will continue to beckon us further and further, and the internet offers an endless road of pornographic scenery.

Viewers of pornography are not innocent passive consumers but active participants creating demand for an industry that preys on others.

Next, when we use our power to access sex, we are always the perpetrator. This is the case with pornography. This isn't the place to present a complete case that pornography is unethical and immoral in and of itself, but it is notable that pornography is most often created at the expense of those involved, using drugs and manipulation. The men and women who are viewed as "actors" are often not eager participants in what is an unrealistic fantasy. David, with all his power, explored his desire with a simple command, and we do the same when we click, swipe, and tap on our devices. Thus, viewers of pornography are not innocent passive consumers but active participants creating demand for an industry that preys on others.

Finally, once we have pursued our desires, we, like David, try to hide our sin. It's common for people who view pornography or participate in an online illicit relationship to clear their web-history and attempt to wipe all evidence of it. This is all the more so the case for those who are caught in their sin by a boss, parent, or spouse. Then follows the pattern of denials and excuses.

The pattern of desire is a familiar one, and you've probably found yourself in it. If so, I don't mean to add to your guilt and shame. That would be neither my nor God's desire. Rather, my objective is to provide understanding combined with hope. There was hope for David and there is hope for you. Desire has a pattern, but so does healing, and you can follow that pattern today.

The Familiar Pattern of Healing

The story ends in 2 Samuel 12 as David's sin is exposed by the prophet Nathan (we'll cover that in the next chapter). David is confronted, and he begins the process of healing and forgiveness. Healing and holiness in this area is possible, and it has often followed the same road.

The pattern of healing begins with confession. David confesses before God and turns his heart in repentance. True, healing confession is always detailed. It is detailed not to build guilt or shame but to make room for full freedom. As humans we tend to downplay our transgressions to ourselves and others. By admitting and confessing to God the full weight of our sin, we begin to realize our need for God's grace and we are able to fully turn away from it and turn instead toward Jesus in repentance.

The next step is riskier, but I guarantee that it is worth it. There is power in exposing our sin to the light and confessing it to another person. As James 5:16a says, "Therefore confess your sins to each other and pray for each other so that you may be healed." To be clear, you do not have to confess to another human being to receive God's forgiveness (1 John 1:9); however, there is definite healing potential in confessing it to another human being. One of the many blessings of confessing your sins to another person is the power of hearing them proclaim the truth of God's forgiveness over you.

After you have confessed, move to repentance and ask for God's help to walk in holiness and health. You can't change your life and your habits on your own. You need God's help, and God desires to help you. God doesn't want you to strive; God wants you to surrender. James 4:6b says, "God opposes the proud but shows favour to the humble." Simply and regularly ask God to help you, seeking God's empowerment and guidance to pursue health and holiness. It will be a long road ahead, but God wants to walk it with you.

In addition to asking for God's help, it is vital that you get the help of another person you trust. I have rarely seen anyone overcome habitual pornography use without the help of others in their life. Years ago, a friend confessed their habitual viewing of pornography to a group I was in. My friend was immensely broken as his spouse had uncovered his secret. I had never seen him so raw and vulnerable. Our group prayed for him and supported him. Over the subsequent months, not only did he find restoration and healing, but several others in our group did as well. It was beautiful! Sin is horrible, but sin exposed in the sanitizing light of God's love brings life, healing, and love. Confessing in community is worth the risk!

There is power in exposing our sin to the light and confessing it to another person.

Confessing in community can move you to accountability. I have had several accountability relationships over the years and, because I know I am always susceptible to certain patterns of sin in my life, I have friends who regularly ask me about it (just as I ask them). We've used code words or phrases to help with phone calls or restaurant conversations, but the intent and impact is the same. Having someone else check in on you can help you to stem an action or thought process or to avoid patterns or places that lead to temptation.

It is important to note that pornography use or illicit online relationships can be a symptom of a greater issue. These deep issues can vary but include: issues of shame, issues of intimacy, lack of self-worth, loneliness, lack of forgiveness, and unresolved anger. Many people who feel chained by pornography cannot break the chains and find healing without first addressing these underlying areas of deep emotional wounding and brokenness. These issues are not easily fixed, and often they need to be addressed comprehensively with the help of a trained counsellor. As you talk with a trusted friend, it may be worth exploring the possibility of seeing a counsellor or psychologist who could help you to work through any deep issues that might be at the root of your pornography use or pursuit of online illicit relationships. If this is a deep-rooted issue in your life, it will take time to dig it out, and you will need help. There is never shame in seeking the help of a trained professional and the support of a trusted friend.

God doesn't want you to strive; God wants you to surrender.

A Hope-Filled Vision of Healing in the Age of Kings

Even though as followers of Jesus we are called to be on mission with Him, we, like King David, can instead be distracted, leverage our power, and pursue our desires. As we learn to follow Jesus in our social media world, with the newfound power of kings and queens, may we find hope and healing together in community, and may we share that hope with the world.

In our digital world, pornography use and illicit online relationships are major issues, but the Church is in a unique position to help people find healing and wholeness. Like Jesus protected the woman caught in adultery, may the Church provide a safe place of healing as we help people "go and sin no more." (John 8:11)

Jesus wants to set the captives free. What if the church were known as the place where guilt and shame were replaced by love and freedom, and hope and healing? What if the church were a place where true healing could occur, where hope could be expressed, and where grace could thrive in the context of unconditional love?

A Royal Reflection

Read
- Psalm 51
- This psalm was written by King David after he was confronted by the prophet Nathan.

Reflect
- How do you struggle with lust in this age of kings and queens?

- Have you ever confessed your sin of lust to someone you trusted? If so, what happened? If not, why not?
- If this is something you struggle with, consider someone you know whom you can talk to and confess your sin to.

Respond

- Read Psalm 51 again. This time, use it to guide your prayer of confession to Jesus and to remind you of His forgiveness.
- Find a community in which to confess and be authentic. Pray and ask God to show you one or more people to whom you can be honest about your struggles. Ask God for courage, and talk to them.
- If this is a major issue in your life, consider seeing a professional to help you work through the deeper issues that might be at the heart of it. If this issue has been part of your life for years, it will take time to work through. Seek help! Healing is possible!

COGNIFICATION

The morning routine isn't quite what it used to be. For instance, consider how someone like me might start the day with the help of all the emerging tools at my disposal.

At the conclusion of a restful night's sleep monitored by a smartwatch and some apps, these same devices process the data from my sleep-cycle and determine the optimal moment to wake me up within a predetermined window of time. When that moment arrives, my favourite wake-up song gently stirs me out of my dreamlike state.

Upon waking, I open up the Bible app on my phone. The app, with the help of algorithms and artificial intelligence that have gauged my physical and mental wellbeing, selects an appropriate Bible verse to give me a sense of hope and purpose for the day ahead. It overlays the verse on a photo I took recently, which was also chosen based on data the app gathered from me.

After my Bible reading, I open up my favorite social media feeds to scroll through the pictures and posts curated by the site's hidden algorithms. I get updates from my friends and from organizations I follow, and I skim over ads that are made for and targeted at people like me.

From there, I log in to my favourite online store to track a purchase I made the day before. My item is shipping quickly because, based on my order history, the site's predictive algorithms made sure the item was shipped to my local warehouse a week ago in anticipation of my predicted purchase. After clicking on a few items suggested specifically for me based on my search history, location, gender, and purchase history, I find the perfect shirt in the perfect size at a price I can't pass up, and I buy it with a single click.

Thinking of getting out of bed, I check the local weather. If it's less than ideal, I impulsively do a quick web search for cheap flights to somewhere warm. Based on my email, search history, and location, the results show me what I mostly likely want to find, along with some results advertisers want me to see. Once I've exhausted the vacation fantasy, I finally get out of bed to find that the air in my house is the ideal temperature — automatically controlled according to my custom settings.

Notice how much of my day, even before my feet have touched the floor, has already been mediated by machines. The digital age is filled with tools both visible and hidden that are engineered to meet our needs and anticipate our desires. This is all thanks to cognification.

Age of Cognification

This Age of Kings is an age of *cognification*. This word refers to the process of making machines progressively "smarter" with the help of artificial intelligence and predictive algorithms.

Cognification employs three tactics: confirmation, anticipation, and gratification. For the purpose of confirmation, smart machines and social media are designed to analyze, predict, and confirm pre-existing beliefs, patterns, and behaviours. By design, smart machines and media are not intended simply to meet our desires, but also to anticipate them. Cognified machines seek to give us what we want before we even know we want it. Based on a misguided understanding of what it means to serve, cognified machines are also engineered to gratify our desires, and to do so without question or judgement.

The digital age is filled with tools both visible and hidden that are engineered to meet our needs and anticipate our desires.

Consider the typical morning I described above. Did you notice that none of the technology in that scenario confronted me about my desires? This is not accidental; it is by design. Smart machines and the media that run on them are designed to serve us — giving/telling us what we want even before we ask for it. Having so many things in our service gives us a power once held only by kings and queens. Picture that morning routine again, but this time imagine that it is a king or queen who is awakened at the perfect time by servants who tell them what they want to hear, anticipate their every need, and gratify their every desire.

Throughout history, all people of great power struggled with this reality. They were surrounded by servants whose sole focus was to confirm, anticipate, and gratify their desires. As a result, those in power have often been placed in an echo chamber that reverberates their ideas and perspectives without ever challenging them, opposing them, or even suggesting that they think critically about them.

It takes great courage to question the perspectives of those in power. Conversely, it takes great courage and humility to listen to divergent voices when we are accustomed to having our own opinions confirmed so consistently. As a result, kings and queens are faced with the temptation to stay in the comfortable arms of confirmation rather than to explore new ideas and contradictory perspectives.

Our Royal Past and Our Royal Present

Danger lurks within the echo chamber of the royal throne room. The greatest kings and queens have realized that they need people within their sphere who will speak truth to their power, who will confront their destructive behaviour, and who will challenge their assumptions.

Historically, this was one of the roles of the court jester. In addition to providing the royal house with entertainment, the court jester was also employed to speak **Cognified** hard truths to the throne. When the servants **machines** of the king and queen were afraid to speak the **seek to give** truth and to confront their rulers with the hard **us what** news of the day, the court jester took on that **we want** sometimes-hazardous responsibility. In our **before we** social media world, where we are all crowned **even know** as kings and queens, who will be our court **we want it.** jesters, willing to tell us the truths that we are inclined to ignore?

Technology is good at anticipating our needs and gratifying our wants, but what if what we want is not what we need? What if what we do is not in our own or in our society's best interest? Will emerging technology ever challenge us to try new things, explore new ideas, or test our preconceived notions?

Who will speak truth to your power? To whom will you grant access to your echo chamber so that they might speak prophetically to you, challenging your ideas, choices, beliefs, behaviours, and perspectives? You can see that our cognified future has much to learn from its royal past.

David's Story Is Our Story

As we examine what it means to pursue God's heart in a social media world, the story of what happens shortly after King David has sex with Bathsheba and murders her husband is specifically relevant. King David is faced with the temptation to ignore the prophetic voice that confronts the destruction he has caused by gratifying his selfish desires. Although he is tempted to block out the voice of the prophet Nathan, David chooses instead to embrace the difficult truth that the prophet proclaims, and this leads the king to repent and restore his relationship with God.

Learning from the Life of King David
2 Samuel 12:1–13

After David sleeps with Bathsheba and has her husband Uriah killed, the narrative ends with the pronouncement, "But the thing David had done displeased the Lord" (2 Samuel 11:27b). The next chapter begins with God moving: "The Lord sent Nathan to David" (2 Samuel 12:1a). After David's most notorious sin, God calls the prophet Nathan to confront David. God does not abandon David to his gross disobedience. Rather, God pursues David and sends someone to confront his sin so that he may return to obedience.

It is important to acknowledge the severity of the risk for Nathan. The task of confronting an all-powerful king with a difficult message is not for the faint of heart. People who confront and challenge kings and queens are often met with severe repercussions, and yet Nathan, in obedience, follows God's leading into the throne room of the king.

It should also be noted that although King David has all the power endowed to him, as evidenced in his behaviours with Bathsheba, he is still willing to listen to Nathan. Even in his sin, David allows Nathan into his throne room to speak truth to his power.

Danger lurks within the echo chamber of the royal throne room.

Nathan first addresses David's sin indirectly, with the help of a parable. Notice that he doesn't simply proclaim his message out of context; rather, Nathan helps David see and discover the truth for himself by sharing a story of injustice. Nathan helps David see the injustice of his behaviour by sharing a story of injustice committed by someone else. Too often, our awareness of injustice — like our awareness of sin — is farsighted: we can see it in others but are blind to it in our own lives. This is hypocrisy. Nathan exposes the hypocrisy of David's outrage through the parable, and David is convicted.

In an about-face from his previous destructive behaviour, David becomes willing not only to hear a confrontational voice, but also to listen and respond to it with deep repentance and change. He accepts responsibility and the severity of the consequences.

Pursuing God's Heart in a Social Media World

In this Age of Kings, who will speak truth to your power? When your opinions and desires are being constantly confirmed with the help of algorithms and like-minded followers, who will be your Nathan? Conversely, for whom will you be a Nathan? For whom will you embrace all the risks of confrontation in order to speak truth to their power?

The Forge of Confrontation

Day after day, technology is conditioning us to believe that the voice of confirmation is the voice of community, but true friendship and community are forged in the furnace of confrontation and friction. As Proverbs 27:17 says, "As iron sharpens iron, so one person sharpens another." This metaphor is often used to illustrate a friendship that is built upon encouragement and affirmation; however, iron doesn't sharpen iron with encouragement and affirmation. That sharpening comes from friction, sparks, and heat. In our emerging age of cognification, we are trying to sharpen our lives with the fine silk of confirmation rather than with the coarse iron of confrontation.

Relationships forged by conflict and challenge can cut deep into the heart and last for a lifetime. These types of relationship are rare, but God uses them to shape us. I have been fortunate enough to have several of these relationships in my life. Several years ago, I was going through a very difficult personal time and a good friend wrote me an email that included some hard truths that I desperately needed to hear. It was difficult to read, but God used it to pull me out of a rut of negative thinking. My good friend risked our relationship to challenge me, and God used his confrontation powerfully in my life.

When we are constantly hearing voices of confirmation, we need to intentionally cultivate relationships in our lives that are not designed to confirm, anticipate, and gratify our desires, opinions, and perspectives. If we want to grow as followers of Jesus, to grow in holiness, and to pursue all that God has for us, we need to intentionally give Nathans a place in our throne room.

The Sawmill of Confrontation

As kings and queens, not only do we need to have people who will speak truth to our power, but we need to be equipped to perform that role for others. We are not accustomed to cultivating relationships that confront. Thus, we struggle even with the kind of healthy confrontation that exudes both truth and love. As Warren Wiersbe notes, "Truth without love is brutality, and love without truth is hypocrisy." [29]

Jesus addresses this in the Sermon on the Mount using imagery from woodshops and sawmills (which he knew well, as a carpenter). Using the image of helping someone remove a speck of sawdust from their eye, Jesus teaches how to use truth and humility to help someone who is sinning.

Why do you look at the speck of sawdust in your brother's eye and pay no attention to the plank in your own eye? How can you say to your brother, 'Let me take the speck out of your eye,' when all the time there is a plank in your own eye? You hypocrite, first take the plank out of your own eye, and then you will see clearly to remove the speck from your brother's eye. (Matthew 7:3–5)

This metaphor is often used to teach that we shouldn't "judge" others because we each have our own issues. In other words, we shouldn't help or confront anyone who is sinning because we're all sinners, too. This line of thinking is flawed, and it leaves us all with itchy eyes and obstructed vision.

If we want to grow as followers of Jesus, to grow in holiness, and to pursue all that God has for us, we need to intentionally give Nathans a place in our throne room.

Have you ever had a literal speak of dust in your eye? It's horrible! Whenever this has happened to me, I've eventually sought someone I trusted to help. I sought a parent, spouse, or friend to look and see what I couldn't and asked them to help me remove it. Additionally, in times when I have seen others struggling with a literal speck in their eye, I have always offered to help. Therefore, before we look into the rest of Jesus' words, we need to recognize that Jesus isn't advocating that we ignore each other's specks and planks of sin; rather, Jesus calls us to courageously and humbly help each other. Thus, the issue Jesus is addressing is not whether we should help remove specks of sin, but how to do it well.

As Jesus teaches, humility is vital for this. We need to recognize that not only do we have our own specks, but we have our own planks. In other words, we should help not from a position of power and privilege but from a position of mutual dependence. Humility allows us to see clearly, and it also helps us to effectively help others.

In the sawmill of confrontation, addressing the truth of someone's sin with the humility of our own should be done on the basis of love and relationship. When I've had a speck of dust in my eye, I've never sought out a stranger to help me remove it. As we lovingly confront those we know, may we always do so in the context of relationship and love.

Finally, as we practice healthy confrontation, it is always important to find the right time and place. Removing specks in public might not be, and rarely is, the best approach. Ask God for wisdom as you help remove the specks in the eyes of others. Remember, if you're going to put your finger in someone else's eye, you're going to need their trust. Both of you will feel vulnerable and unsure. The same is true when you confront someone in their sin. Always cultivate mutual trust and vulnerability before you start poking!

> **Humility allows us to see clearly, and it also helps us to effectively help others.**

The Cultivation of Confrontation

As we forge our relationships through confrontation and help each other with humility in the sawmill, we also cultivate our relationships in the garden of difference. In an age of cognification where we are prone to build communities mediated by our individual preferences, we need to cultivate relationships with diverse people. In the age of cognification, we have a distinct temptation to cultivate communities made up only of people who think like us and who tend to con-firm our perspectives, share the same ideas, have the same political leaning, be of similar social standing, and laugh at the same jokes. However, if all of our relationships are with people who are just like us, how can we learn to truly love? If everyone we love is just like us, does that mean that we only love ourselves?

When the Bible defines love in 1 Corinthians 13:4–7, it uses words like patience, kindness, protection, trust, perseverance, and hope. Although this passage is often quoted at weddings and in the context of romantic love, the actual context is of a church in the midst of chaos and conflict, including major theological differences. This description of love in the Bible is not just for those we like and get along with; it is for those we disagree with, dislike, and even despise.

Sound impossible? It is! At least with only our own strength. This is why many of the descriptions of love in 1 Corinthian 13 are also shared with the Fruit of the Spirit in Galatians 5. God desires to strengthen and empower us with the Holy Spirit so that we can love the different and difficult.

Do you know and love people who have different theo-logical views than you, different political ideologies than you, and different worship preferences than you? Do your social media feeds represent people with different opinions and ideas than you? Are you guilty of unfollowing, unfriending, hiding, and blocking everyone and everything you disagree with? Through social media, have you created an echoing throne room devoid of confrontation?

You might need to hide, unfollow, and unfriend people who are toxic and divisive, but don't hide those who simply hold divergent views and values. Ask God for wisdom, and check your heart, so that you can recognize the difference. Too many of us hide first and ask questions later. It's all too easy to stop seeing posts from that distant relative of yours with those different political views, but is that the right response? If you're going to learn how to love and practice love as a follower of Jesus, you need to come face to face with divergent opinions and different ways of life. Your social media feed should be less like a carefully tended garden of sameness and more like a practice field of difference, where you can learn to love the diverse people who live in the world.

This is where a social media "sameness audit" can be highly valuable. This is the process of checking your social media feeds, friends, and followers to make sure you haven't stacked your throne room with people who agree with you. Take time and go through your friends lists, news feeds, and lists of people you follow, and see how much they reflect you, your desires, and your perspectives. Seek diversity in your social media circles and intentionally allow in more voices that require you to practice patience and understanding. This will, in turn, push you to lean on God.

If you only cultivate relationships of agreement, you, like farms that only produce the same crop every year, have a greater potential for disease and destructiveness. Your life will begin to rot if you hear only the melody of sameness and don't listen for the harmony of difference. This harmony is at the core of healthy community and Christian discipleship.

My fellow royals, although we are surrounded by servants made of technology, may we intentionally cultivate diverse relationships, forge them in the fire of confrontation, and help each other remove our specks of sin with humility. For the health of our souls, may we invite prophets into our throne rooms and may we humbly listen, and speak the truth, and do it all drenched in love.

A Hope-Filled Vision of Confrontation in the Age of Kings

As king and queens in the cognified world, when we are inundated with confirmations that seek to anticipate and gratify our desires, may we allow others to speak truth to our power. May we intentionally invite those who disagree with us and are different from us into our throne rooms and demonstrate to our social media age that confrontation is not something to be avoided but rather to be embraced. By God's design, the Church has — and *is* — a prophetic message for a culture of sameness. In our social media age, may we be a people of diverse opinions and different perspectives, centred around Jesus. In a world that fosters sameness as a virtue, the Church has a unique and appealing voice.

Your life will begin to rot if you hear only the melody of sameness and don't listen for the harmony of difference.

As we move forward into this emerging reality, may we, as the Church, be known for our love (John 13:35). May the church be a people and place where truth is spoken to power with love and received with grace. Confrontation is not something to be avoided; rather, confrontation is a gift that's worthy to be embraced if it's done in love.

A Royal Reflection

Read

- Psalm 32
- This is a psalm of praise by David expressing thanksgiving for the forgiveness of sin.

Reflect

- How do you think cognification has affected you?
- Have you ever had a positive experience of confrontation? What made it positive?

- Have you ever had a negative experience of confrontation? What made it negative?
- Why do you think it's important to recognize the plank in your own eye before you can help someone with the speck in theirs? When have you done this?
- Do a social media friendship and follower audit. How diverse is your social media circle? Why do you think it's important for your faith and discipleship to be connected and in relationship with people who are different from you?

Respond

- Who have you invited into your throne room to speak truth to your power?
- What plank might Jesus want you to deal with in your eye?
- Pray and ask God to widen the circle of your friends with increased diversity.

FAKE NEWS

"The wolf is coming!"

The fable of the boy who cried wolf is a story reawakened for our era of social media, information overload, and fake news. This common children's story has ancient roots that reach back thousands of years. A former slave named Aesop recorded this fable among many others during Ancient Greek times, but some of the oral stories recorded could go back as far as the time of David. It's interesting to imagine that David might have heard this story recounted when he was a young shepherd.

In this classic tale, a shepherd boy repeatedly calls for the help of his fellow villagers, telling them that a wolf is attacking his flock. Although his cry for help is fake, the attention he receives is real, and attention is addictive. The boy becomes the centre of attention in his village. His voice is heard, people respond to him, and he feels important. In an effort to keep this experience going, the boy calls for assistance again and again. The villagers grow increasingly annoyed and suspicious at the continued false alarms until eventually they ignore him.

Then, one day, the wolf actually arrives, and it's hungry. The boy cries for help, but no one listens. His voice is ignored, and his sheep are killed by the ravenous wolf. In fact, in some versions of the story, the boy dies along with his sheep, trying to protect them.

The moral of Aesop's fable is simple: always tell the truth. If you don't, when you need people to believe you, they won't.

On social media and in contemporary news coverage, we hear voices crying wolf day in and day out. These websites are all in competition with each other to get clicks, views, and impressions, and so each one tries to cry more loudly than the others. They are in a relentless race for our attention, and they don't particularly care if their cries ring true. Like the shepherd, the ever-increasing calls of fake news, fake websites, clickbait, and camouflaged satire deceptively seek our attention with empty exaggerations, half-truths, and full-out lies. And, like the villagers in the story, we are fooled at first, but eventually we become skeptical and apathetic.

In a sea of perplexing information, it is easier to evaluate the information we are confronted with through our preconceived ideas and perspectives.

In an era of endless information, some of which is true, some of which is false, and much of which is somewhere in the middle, we can lose the capacity to discern what's what. Our truth-filters wear thin to the point that we ignore the question, or simply believe what we think should be true rather than what actually is.

In a sea of perplexing information, it is easier to evaluate the information we are confronted with through our pre-conceived ideas and perspectives. Additionally, as kings and queens who have the ability and power to decide what to believe, sometimes it is just easier to believe what makes us feel better and doesn't confront our pre-existing notions and personal narratives.

Fake News, Confirmation Bias, and Intentional Information Avoidance

Fake news has become an epidemic in our time. Because it takes time to discern truth from falsehood, many of us simply avoid discernment altogether. There are those who have taken advantage of this avoidance in order to peddle stories and information that seem real at first glance but are not — fake news. These stories are designed to deceive us or distract us from what's really going on.

Consider Pizzagate, a conspiracy theory that circulated during the 2016 United States presidential election. The conspiracy claimed that an email published by WikiLeaks unveiled a human trafficking child-sex ring run by Hillary Clinton and the democratic party. [30] Belief in the story eventually led an armed man to enter a pizza parlor in a misguided attempt to rescue children. Because of their strong hatred for the Clinton family, many people took this fake news as fact; the story aligned with a narrative that they believed deeply.

Although most adults are aware of and concerned about fake news, surprisingly few can actually spot it. A Pew Research poll found that the vast majority of adults (about 85 percent) believe they can spot and detect fake news, [31] while an Ipsos Public Affairs and Buzzfeed poll found that 75 percent of adults are fooled by fake news headlines.[32] We know it is a problem, we are aware it exists, and yet we are still fooled by it.

Our propensity to believe fake news comes from phenomena known as *confirmation bias* and *intentional information avoidance*. Confirmation bias is the phenomenon of evaluating what is true by what confirms our pre-existing perspectives and narratives. Because confirmation bias can prove to be an efficient means of quickly and subconsciously sifting through endless information, we can rely on it so comprehensively that it can be used against us. As a result, we can believe things that are not true but that sound, at least to us, like they are.

Intentional information avoidance is also a factor as we navigate all the information we are constantly confronted with. Intentional information avoidance is the conscious action of avoiding information, particularly information that challenges something we are comfortable believing in.

In *Being Wrong: Adventures in the Margins of Error*, Kathryn Schulz asks the provocative question, "What does it feel like to be wrong?"[33] One instinctively answers with words like *uncomfortable*, *embarrassing*, or *shameful*. These are, in Shultz's estimation, good answers, but to the wrong question. These answer the question of what it feels like to *find out* you are wrong. So, what does it actually feel like to *be* wrong? Exactly the same as it feels to be right.

No one wants to feel uncomfortable, embarrassed, or ashamed, so we intentionally avoid information that would challenge our understanding of truth and norms, even when it has intellectual or factual merit. You might be tempted to cast this off as an issue for others, but if you simply evaluate your own social media habits you will probably see your own propensity for this.

In a fake news era, media outlets, political parties, and misguided individuals feed off of our confirmation biases and intentional information avoidance. They use them to manipulate their followers, propagate their ideas, and push their agendas.

Astroturfing

Fake news exists alongside fake reviews. We've grown accustomed to reading reviews online when we need to pick between contractors, restaurants, churches, university professors, and even doctors. Reviews exist everywhere and there is a common perception that because they are crowd-sourced at a grassroots level by seemingly independent users, they can be trusted.

The reality is not so simple. Consider a phenomenon called *astroturfing*. Companies pay online bloggers and social media personalities to review products or features through their personal posts in an effort to make the review seem authentic. In an effort to draw attention to these kinds of practices, Oobah Butler used his experience as a paid fake restaurant reviewer to trick TripAdvisor into making his non-existent restaurant the top-rated restaurant in London. [34] The same is true of bloggers who post glowing reviews of products that they have received for free or with direct or indirect compensation, conveniently neglecting to tell their readers about their inherent conflict of interest.

In a more sinister version of this, companies have been

known to pay people to write negative reviews of their competitors. In response, various corporations have now deployed reputation-management teams to help proactively manage their social media presence and their reputations online.

Fake news and fake reviews have exploited our biases, making the truth and accuracy of information difficult to evaluate and discern.

David's Story Is Our Story

Kings and queens throughout history have carried the unique responsibility to discern truth from among the various voices that compete for their attention. This responsibility is now in everyone's hand, and it takes time and practice to learn to carry it. Part of this practice includes understanding and compensating for our confirmation bias and intentional information avoidance. These have always been challenges for kings and queens, including King David.

Learning from the Life of King David
2 Samuel 18:19–33

In the story, after the prophet Nathan confronts King David, some family dysfunction leads David's son Absalom to lead a coup against his father and take control of the Kingdom of Israel.

The revolt eventually comes to an end when David, fortified in nearby Mahanaim, sends his men to fight against the Israelite army that is being led by Absalom. As David gives the order to his commanders (including Joab), he explicitly instructs them to be gentle with Absalom (2 Samuel 18:5). Absalom is still David's son, and he loves him.

As David's army conquers Israel's army in the forest of Ephraim, Absalom ends up in the hands of Joab who, in defiance of David's orders, kills him.

With Absalom dead and his army defeated, it is time to give David the news. Ahimaaz, the named and known messenger, enthusiastically volunteers to run and tell David the good news of victory, but Joab denies his request. Joab knows that if Ahimaaz tells David the bad news of Absalom's death, it could end in his harm or his death (see 2 Samuel 1:15). Therefore, Joab asks an unnamed Cushite to run to the gates and tell David everything he has seen.

In a fake news era, media outlets, political parties, and misguided individuals feed off of our confirmation biases and intentional information avoidance.

Shortly after the Cushite leaves, Ahimaaz pleads to follow him, and Joab lets him go. As they both run to Mahanaim, Ahimaaz outruns the Cushite and ends up at the city's outer gates first to tell David the news. Ahimaaz is recognized and because he is known as a good man and is travelling alone (in the text it is assumed that travelling alone indicates news of victory in battle), David assumes the news will be good — that his army has won and that his son is safe.

Ahimaaz tells David the good news about the victory. When David asks about Absalom, Ahimaaz, unaware of specifics and probably afraid to give the difficult news, recoils in fear of sharing the bad news. At this time, the Cushite arrives. The Cushite tells David about the victory, and when David asks about his son, the Cushite instantly replies with the news of Absalom's death. The Cushite thinks both are good news, but, of course, David does not. His victory in battle is overshadowed by the death of his son.

This story provides fascinating insight into King David's mind as he attempts to process the news from the war. As the separate runners arrive, David assumes two things that kings and queens of his time would also have assumed: First, because Ahimaaz and the Cushite were running alone, they must be carrying good news (2 Samuel 18:25, 26); second, because it was from someone (a source) he believed to be good, the news must be true and trustworthy (2 Samuel 18:27). As we discover in the narrative, the news in both cases is more complex than simply "good," and the "good man" didn't share the whole story.

In our age of kings and queens, we are given the power to discern and control the news and information we hear and respond to. As a result, we, too, can be influenced by confirmation bias and intentional information avoidance, at times falling victim to those who would manipulate us with fake news that affirms our pre-existing narratives and perspectives.

Pursuing God's Heart in a Social Media World

Sharing news to kings and queens is complicated. They have the power to silence you if you have news they don't want to hear. Therefore, there is a market to customize news to a specific audience. In the life of David, this is seen in

Ahimaaz's hesitation to share the difficult news about Absalom's death. In our social media age, it's seen in the different news sources that compete for our attention so that they can survive in the increasing competitive media environment. Like it or not, our newfound power and the preferences it has given us have created the very fractured media-market we decry.

It's also complicated for kings and queens like me and you to discern truth. How do we know if news is true? Do we even want to know if the news is true? How do we find the truth when so many versions of the "truth" are competing for our attention?

In a sea of information, and with choirs of voices crying wolf, how do we discern and share truth effectively?

Discerning Truth

As we get more and more of our news and information online and through social media, it is vital that we discern between truth and falsehood in the information we are consuming and filter it accordingly.

Just as food critics spend years developing their palates in an effort to distinguish gourmet food made with high-quality ingredients from foods made with artificial ingredients, we need to develop our palates for truth in a world that's saturated with information. As we train our information-palates to discern correctly, it is vital to identify the six things that aid us to discern truth in an era of fake news.

First, **smell it.** Smell has a distinct connection to our sense of taste and can help us in our initial assessment. When you see a post, article, video, or meme, ask yourself some initial questions. Is it satire (a surprising number of people have experienced instant outrage at a post, posing as news, when it was really satire)? Does it sound too good to be true (is it playing off your confirmation bias)? Does the headline sound overly provocative (a technique used by clickbait to get you to read something)? Does it look like part of a larger story (stories presented out of their full context can be misleading)?

Second, *check the ingredients.* Any food critic with a discerning palate knows that fresh organic ingredients always create the best food. Thus, when you are faced with news, posts, videos, or memes, ask the following questions. What are the underlying facts that it is based on (are they from a reputable source)? Is there a scientific study referenced to prove the solution presented (choosing your cancer treatment based on something you read on someone's blog is not the best medical advice)? What statistics are they using?

Third, *check the source.* Food connoisseurs know that where ingredients come from makes all the difference. As you evaluate the information shared on social media, check its source. First, look at the web address or original social media account it comes from. Is it from a trusted and legitimate source? If you have any concerns or even a suspicion, do a quick check with a fact-checking service online (several exist). Check if the source has a known bias or agenda they are propagating, and consider whether this might affect or influence the information they are giving you.

Fourth, *taste it.* Food critics know to look past the description and presentation and taste the food. Once you've smelled it, inspected the ingredients, and looked at the source, read it and think about it. Truth will always stand the test of examination and reflection. Ask, does it align with the other facts that you know to be true? If not, explore why not. If so, do a sober second thought and double-check if your confirmation bias or your intentional information avoidance tendencies might be at work.

Fifth, *discuss it.* Truth tends to withstand cross-examination by the community, while fake news does not. The multiple perspectives provided by diverse people help us to see things differently, to ask different questions, and to discern more accurately. Therefore, what if instead of using social media to post with confidence, we used it to discern? What if we were to post a meme **Social media could use more question marks and fewer exclamation marks.** with a question (Is this true?) rather than a pronouncement (This is true!). Social media could use more question marks and fewer exclamation marks.

Sixth, *savor it.* If it is true, savor it. Truth should always take time to process. Allow the new information you have gathered to digest slowly, and see whether it challenges your preconceived ideas and perspectives or affirms your convictions. Remember, truth doesn't cower from critical reflection and examination; rather, truth dances with joy in their presence.

Sharing Truth

In our fake news world, most people have unintentionally (and some intentionally) passed along false information. As we mature our collective palates so that they can discern the truth, it is important for us to help each other and avoid propagating fake news. Therefore, when we see it, we should name it and when we share it, we should correct it.

When you see it, name it! Fake and misleading news and information is everywhere. Sometimes it is harmless satire, and sometimes it is intentionally misleading. In an effort to acknowledge that it exists and to train our palates for truth, it is important that we name it when we see it. When you come across a post in your newsfeed that you evaluate as objectively false, it is important to identify it for yourself. It is also important to report it to your social networks and, when appropriate, to lovingly and kindly identify it as such for the person who may have ignorantly and innocently shared it.

When you share it, correct it! We are all susceptible to fake news. It is humbling to get caught in a web of deception that was spun by fake news. When you are, it is important to identify it, correct it, apologize for it, and move on. As you are confronted with fake news, may you do your part to discern, embrace, and promote a healthy diet of good information that is rooted in truth.

Embracing Truth

Truth is never something to run away from, but always towards.

It's becoming increasingly common for people to label any unflattering news or news they disagree with *fake news*. In order to avoid cognitive dissonance and the implications of the information that has been presented to them, a person can confidently deny its truthfulness and end all conversation. When unflattering or uncomfortable truth confronts us, it can be tempting to label it as fake news so that we don't have to grapple with it. But when our core beliefs are unsubstantiated and we avoid any truths that challenge us, we are living in a false version of reality. And however comfortable that reality might be, it will eventually come crashing down with the smallest of breezes, like a house of cards. May we always remind ourselves that truth is never something to run away from, but always towards.

A Hope-Filled Vision of Truth in the Age of Kings

As kings and queens in the age of fake news, it is vital that we have the ability to discern the truth. Furthermore, as followers of Jesus who know that Jesus is the way, the truth, and the life (John 14:6), we know that truth is important even if it makes us uncomfortable or challenges our existing conceptions and established beliefs. Pursuing God's heart in a social media world means always pursuing and embracing truth, no matter where we find it and no matter how it makes us feel.

Imagine if the church and God's people were known as loving and kind truth-seekers in our culture. Imagine if everything we posted, commented on, and shared online were filled with truth and drenched in love. Imagine if social media were saturated with Jesus-followers who embodied both grace and truth (John 1:14). That would be revolutionary!

A Royal Reflection

Read

- Psalm 3
- David wrote this psalm after he fled from his son Absalom.

Reflect

- Have you ever read, believed, or shared fake news? How did it happen?
- How can you grow in awareness of your confirmation bias and inclination to intentional information avoidance?

- What part of your palate for truthful information needs the most maturing? What can you do today to mature your palate to discern truth?

Respond

- As you use your social media accounts this week, commit to believing, acting on, and sharing only the information and news that you have intentionally discerned.
- Read Psalm 3 again. In a world of fake news, how important is it that we don't listen to false voices that will tell us things like "God will not deliver him" (3:2) but instead hear the truth that "from the Lord comes deliverance" (3:8)?
- Pray and ask God to help you embrace social media as not simply a means to share information but a platform to express the good news of Jesus' Kingdom.

King David's Last Words

HOPE AND LIFE IN THE AGE OF KINGS

As our world vibrates with the frequency of change, how will we respond?

David was not only a shepherd, a warrior, and a king; he was also a gifted musician and songwriter. David was known for his ability to play the harp or lyre in a way that soothed the troubled King Saul (1 Samuel 16). David had the skill to make beautiful music from vibrating strings.

What if we learned to pursue God in a way that would bring the beauty of Jesus' kingdom into our social media age? If we learned to play music with our lives — through our social media activity and in our Christian communities — we, like David, could soothe our troubled world, bringing life and healing.

If there is hope for King David, there is hope for kings and queens like you and me.

As our world matures from its infancy in the social media age, we, as followers of Jesus, have a unique opportunity to lead the way in helping our world adjust, stand, walk, and run with its newfound royal power. Imagine what could become possible if we leveraged the power granted by social media for God's mission and pursued His heart in our broken world.

Near the end of his life and reign, King David, the royal musician, composed these inspired poetic words as recorded in 2 Samuel 23:2–4:

> *"The Spirit of the Lord spoke through me;*
> *his word was on my tongue.*
> *The God of Israel spoke,*
> *the Rock of Israel said to me:*
> *'When one rules over people in righteousness,*
> *when he rules in the fear of God,*
> *he is like the light of morning at sunrise*
> *on a cloudless morning,*
> *like the brightness after rain that*
> *brings grass from the earth.'"*

David's last words hold deep meaning and convey a hopeful vision for our age of kings and queens. As a king after God's own heart, David reminds himself and the future kings of Israel that if they rule with righteousness and fear God, they will be blessed. I believe that this vision also applies to us as kings and queens in our social media world.

Most articles, books, and blogs that analyze social media do so with a good deal of rebuke and condemnation; social media is often discussed with a measure of dread, as if it were devoid of any hope or possibility. I trust that you've found that this book has a very different tone. Although it recognizes the challenges and the darker side of social media, it does so with profound hope that social media does hold other, better possibilities.

As newly crowned kings and queens thrust onto unfamiliar thrones, we're still learning how to stand, let alone walk, under the weight of our crowns. As we learn, we will continue to stumble and wobble, and we'll carry bruises as a result, but the journey is long; the failures that wound us along the way are only a small part of the journey. There is so much possibility for kings and queens who pursue God's heart. I know that with the right training we will be able to run.

Imagine what could become possible if we leveraged the power granted by social media for God's mission and pursued His heart in our broken world.

As followers of Jesus, may we stand tall and reach further, running on mission together, empowered by the opportunities and abilities that social media provides. As we do, may we discover our true identity, conquer giants, experience true friendship, share life with our words, give all glory to God, walk in sexual wholeness, embrace humility, and seek truth together.

This is where the promise and hope of David's last words are so poignant. When the powerful wield their power righteously and live in a way that honours God, life springs forth.

With more and more people living more and more of their lives on social media, will we live Jesus' glorious mission everywhere, all the time? As our world continues to wrestle with and adapt to social media, a technology that democratizes and decentralizes power, we can be a shining light. Therefore, as we log into our social media platforms, may we carry David's hope-filled blessing, and may we engage our new world with the grace and truth of Jesus.

If there is hope for King David, there is hope for kings and queens like you and me.

NOTES

[1] For my doctoral program, I studied the impact of social media on preaching, and in my academic teaching and various workshops that I lead I've also focused on what it means to faithfully follow Jesus and minister effectively in a digital world.

[2] Author unknown.

[3] Robert Lang introduced this in his TED talk *The Math and Magic of Origami*, February 2008. Available online at https://www.ted.com/talks/robert_lang_folds_way_new_origami

[4] Marshall McLuhan. *Understanding Media: The Extensions of Man.* MIT Press, 1994, pp. 41–42.

[5] "New Beauty Study Reveals Days, Times and Occasions When U.S. Women Feel Least Attractive," CISION PR Newswire, October 2, 2013. Available online at https://www.prnewswire.com/news-releases/new-beauty-study-reveals-days-times-and-occasions-when-us-women-feel-least-attractive-226131921.html

[6] "Jump the Shark" is a reference to a "Happy Days" episode that featured Fonzie literally jumping over a shark on water skis in an attempt to remedy the show's failing popularity. Seen as the point where the popular television show lost its way and began its downward spiral, the phrase is now synonymous with the beginning of the end of something and the desperate attempt to reclaim what was lost.

[7] Markham Heid, "You Asked: Is It Bad for You to Read the News Constantly?" *TIME*, January 31, 2018. Available online at http://time.com/5125894/is-reading-news-bad-for-you/

[8] Brian A. Primack et al., "Social Media Use and Perceived Social Isolation Among Young Adults in the U.S.," *American Journal of Preventive Medicine* 53(1): 1–8. Available online at https://doi.org/10.1016/j.amepre.2017.01.010

[9] Sherry Turkle, *Alone Together: Why We Expect More from Technology and Less from Each Other* (New York: Basic Books, 2011).

[10] Marshal McLuhan and Quentin Fiore, *The Medium Is the Massage: An Inventory of Effects* (Corte Madera: Gingko Press, 2011), 8–9.

[11] Nathaniel Penn, "Buried Alive: Stories From Inside Solitary Confinement," *GQ*, March 2, 2017. Available online at https://www.gq.com/story/buried-alive-solitary-confinement

[12] Mary Murphy Corcoran, "Effect of Solitary Confinement on the Well Being of Prison Inmates," *Applied Psychology OPUS* (Spring 2015). Available online at https://steinhardt.nyu.edu/appsych/opus/issues/2015/spring/corcoran

[13] There is an important side-lesson here for kings and queens who are under threat — from friends and foes alike — in the kingdom. If we find our identity, worth, security, and safety in social acceptance and others' embrace, we will always find ourselves wanting. Therefore, before we seek affirmation from our friends, may we always find confirmation in our identity as children of God and find our calling and destiny in Him.

[14] See https://postsecret.com/

[15] Anne Vandermey, "PostSecret Founder Has a Few Things to Say About New Anonymous Apps," *Fortune*, August 9, 2014. Available online at http://fortune.com/2014/08/09/postsecret-founder-has-a-few-things-to-say-about-new-anonymous-apps/

[16] For more on this, see Chris Baraniuk, "How Twitter Bots Help Fuel Political Feuds," *Scientific American*, March 27, 2018, available online at https://www.scientificamerican.com/article/how-twitter-bots-help-fuel-political-feuds

[17] This is a major shift and softening of the regular fable. In the regular fable the first two goats delay the troll by convincing him to wait for the next goat, promising it will be bigger and tastier, until the third goat appears and, because of his larger size, is able to attack and kill the troll.

[18] See Maria Konnikova's article "The Psychology of Online Comments" in the *New Yorker* for more on how anonymity affects our online behaviour, available online at https://www.newyorker.com/tech/elements/the-psychology-of-online-comments.

[19] See the full survey at http://www.pewinternet.org/2017/07/11/online-harassment-2017/

[20] Lindsay Baker, "Where Does the Red Carpet Come From?" *BBC Culture*, February 22, 2016. Available online at http://www.bbc.com/culture/story/20160222-where-does-the-red-carpet-come-from

[21] Adam Alter, *Irresistible: The Rise of Addictive Technology and the Business of Keeping Us Hooked* (New York: Penguin Press, 2017).

[22] This video captures the sound: https://www.youtube.com/watch?v=qC1oi3N0w_M

[23] You can find the entry here: http://bryceashlinmayo.com/2012/08/mobiquity-part-one-of-three/

[24] Geoff White, "One in Every Thousand Tweets Is Porn," *Channel4 News*. Available online at https://www.channel4.com/news/one-in-every-thousand-tweets-is-porn

[25] Mauro Coletto, Luca Maria Aiello, Claudio Lucchese and Fabrizio Silvestri, "Pornography Consumption in Social Media," from "On the Behaviour of Deviant Communities in Online Social Networks," Proceedings of the 10th International AAAI Conference on Web and Social Media, May 17–20, Cologne, Germany. Available online at https://arxiv.org/pdf/1612.08157.pdf

[26] Jeff Logue, "Pornography Statistics: Who Uses Porn?" *Thought Hub*, October 22, 2015. Available online at https://www.sagu.edu/thoughthub/pornography-statistics-who-uses-pornography

[27] Jason S. Carroll, Laura M. Padilla-Walker, Larry J. Nelson, Chad D. Olson, Carolyn McNamara Barry, and Stephanie D. Madsen, "Generation XXX: Pornography Acceptance and Use Among Emerging Adults," *Journal of Adolescent Research* 23 (2008): 6–30.

[28] I agree with the many commentators who have argued that this act was not consensual and that this is not a story of David's adultery with Bathsheba but, rather, a story of David's rape of Bathsheba.

[29] Warren W. Wiersbe, *On Being a Leader for God* (Grand Rapids, MI: Baker Books, 2011), 39.

[30] Marc Fisher, John Woodrow Cox, and Peter Hermann, "Pizzagate: From Rumor, to Hashtag, to Gunfire in D.C.," *The Washington Post*, December 6, 2016. Available online at https://www.washingtonpost.com/local/pizzagate-from-rumor-to-hashtag-to-gunfire-in-dc/2016/12/06/4c7def50-bbd4-11e6-94ac-3d324840106c_story.html?noredirect=on&utm_term=.a0a2a167989b

[31] Michael Barthel, Amy Mitchell, and Jesse Holcomb, "Many Believe Fake News Is Sowing Confusion," *Pew Research Center*, December 15, 2016. Available online at http://www.journalism.org/2016/12/15/many-americans-believe-fake-news-is-sowing-confusion/

[32] Craig Silverman and Jeremy Singer-Vine, "Most Americans Who See Fake News Believe It, New Survey Says," *Buzzfeed News*, December 6, 2016. See https://www.buzzfeed.com/craigsilverman/fake-news-survey?utm_term=.ybxdvaAle#.rv2o5Ove9

[33] Kathryn Schulz, *Being Wrong: Adventures in the Margin of Error* (New York: HarperCollins, 2010), 18.

[34] Watch the full story at https://www.youtube.com/watch?v=bqPARIKHbN8

ABOUT THE AUTHOR

Bryce Ashlin-Mayo has been married to Laurie for over twenty years and they have three great kids. Bryce has served in full-time pastoral ministry with the Christian and Missionary Alliance in Canada for more than twenty years in a variety of roles. He currently serves as Lead Pastor at Westlife Church in Calgary, Alberta, and teaches sessionally at Ambrose University. Bryce has a Bachelor of Theology from Ambrose University, a Master of Divinity in Pastoral Leadership from Taylor Seminary, and a Doctor of Ministry in Semiotics and Future Studies from George Fox University. Bryce is passionate about seeing people equipped to use technology and social media to advance God's mission.

Connect with Bryce online at bryceashlinmayo.com.

Made in the USA
Middletown, DE
22 February 2019